A *TACKLING TOXICITY* BOOK

Quitting to WIN

GRAHAM MICHAELS

Copyright © 2024 by Graham Michaels

All rights reserved.

No portion of this book may be reproduced in any form without written permission from the publisher or author, except as permitted by U.S. copyright law.

Contents

Introduction: Breaking Free from the Narcissist's Game	1
Part I: Reclaim Control	6
1. The Emotional Trap: Why Narcissists Thrive on Conflict	8
2. Protecting Your Children's Emotional Well-being	18
3. The Guilt of Letting Go: Overcoming Emotional Attachments	30
Part II: Mastering Emotional Freedom	38
4. The E.M.P.O.W.E.R. System: Your Path to Co-parenting Mastery	40
5. Emotions: Regulating Your Reactions	48
6. Mindset: Shifting from Victim to Empowered Co-Parent	62
7. Practices: Building Daily Habits for Strength	75
8. Obstacles: Navigating Legal, Financial, and Emotional Hurdles	86
9. Withdrawal: Detaching Without Disengaging	98

10. Enforcement: Maintaining Boundaries with Confidence	108
11. Resilience: Building Lasting Emotional Strength	118
Part III: Thriving Beyond Co-parenting	129
12. Navigating Major Life Events with Your Narcissistic Ex	131
13. Helping Your Children Build Emotional Resilience	142
14. Maintaining Your Peace When Your Ex Tries to Escalate	164
15. Sustaining Emotional Growth	175
16. Building a Supportive Community	182
17. A Life of Empowerment Beyond the Narcissist	192
Conclusion: Your Path to Lasting Peace	202
I'd Love Your Feedback!	208
References	211

Introduction: Breaking Free from the Narcissist's Game

The struggle of co-parenting with a narcissist is an emotional rollercoaster that takes a toll on every aspect of your life. Your heart aches for your children, watching them navigate the stormy waters of this toxic relationship. You feel the weight of responsibility, the never-ending worry that the narcissist's manipulative behavior will leave lasting scars on their emotional well-being. But there's more—you're also grappling with your own emotional wounds, desperately trying to detach from the narcissist's grip while maintaining your role as a loving and responsible parent. Every text message, every meeting, and every decision becomes an opportunity for your ex to push your buttons and regain control, leaving you feeling powerless.

Yet, there is a way out—a path toward reclaiming your peace and restoring balance in your life. It begins with the power of *detachment*. Detachment isn't about giving up; it's about letting go of and becoming immune to the emotional hooks the narcissist uses to keep you tied to their control.

This book introduces the **E.M.P.O.W.E.R. System**, a 60-day program designed to help you break free from the cycle of conflict and regain control for yourself and your children. By mastering the principles of emotional detachment, you'll discover how to neutralize the narcissist's power over you, creating an environment of peace and stability in your life and in your co-parenting relationship.

The Unseen Emotional Toll of Co-Parenting with a Narcissist

You wake up tired: not just the kind that comes from a lack of sleep, but the kind that reaches deep into your soul. Co-parenting with a narcissist feels like a never-ending emotional marathon. They thrive on drama and conflict, drawing you into battles you didn't even realize you were fighting. Whether it's through constant phone calls, passive-aggressive text messages, or manipulative tactics that turn every decision into a power struggle, the narcissist's goal is to keep you emotionally entangled.

You've likely noticed how the constant tension affects your relationship with your children. Maybe you feel guilty about the emotional impact this toxic environment is having on them. You try to shield them, but how can you protect them when you're struggling to protect yourself? You've heard the phrase "detachment" before, but in the thick of things, it can feel impossible to imagine disengaging from the narcissist's constant provocations.

Yet, detachment is exactly where your strength lies. Detaching emotionally doesn't mean you stop caring about your children or the co-parenting arrangement. It means you stop allowing the narcissist to control your emotional reactions. Detachment is the key to breaking the cycle of conflict, freeing your mind and heart from the narcissist's manipulation, and creating a safe emotional space for your children.

Introducing the 60-Day E.M.P.O.W.E.R. System

This book isn't just about survival—it's about *transformation*. Over the next 60 days, you'll embark on a journey using the E.M.P.O.W.E.R. System, a structured approach that will guide you through the process of reclaiming your emotional freedom and building a healthier co-parenting dynamic. Here's what you can expect:

1. **Emotions**: Learn how to recognize and regulate your emotional triggers. When your ex attempts to provoke you, you'll have the tools to remain calm, composed, and in control.

2. **Mindset**: Shift from feeling like a victim to becoming an empowered co-parent. How you think about yourself, your ex, and your role in your children's lives will change, setting you on a path toward emotional resilience.

3. **Practices**: Develop daily habits that strengthen your emotional fortitude. Mindfulness, journaling, and self-care will become essential tools for maintaining your inner peace amidst the chaos.

4. **Obstacles**: Anticipate and navigate the inevitable legal, financial, and emotional hurdles that arise in co-parenting with a narcissist. You'll learn how to manage these obstacles with confidence and clarity.

5. **Withdrawal**: Master the art of emotional detachment without disengaging from your responsibilities as a parent. You'll learn to create healthy boundaries, communicate effectively, and protect your emotional well-being.

6. **Enforcement**: Enforce boundaries with confidence, ensuring that the narcissist can no longer push you into conflicts that drain your energy and peace.

7. **Resilience**: Build long-term emotional strength for yourself and your children. You'll learn how to model resilience and teach your children emotional regulation, providing them with the tools to navigate their relationship with their narcissistic parent.

Why Detachment is Your Path to Empowerment

Detachment isn't an act of avoidance—it's an act of *empowerment*. It's about recognizing that you can't control the narcissist, but you can control how you respond to them. The narcissist thrives on emotional reactions. Every time you get drawn into a conflict, you feed their hunger for control. By detaching, you take away their power. You stop reacting to their provocations and begin protecting your emotional energy.

This doesn't mean you stop caring about what's best for your children - quite the opposite. In fact, detachment allows you to focus more clearly on their needs. When you're no longer emotionally entangled in the narcissist's manipulation, you can parent from a place of strength and clarity. You're able to make decisions based on what's best for your children, rather than reacting to your ex's toxic behavior.

Detachment is also a form of protection. It shields you from the emotional wounds the narcissist tries to inflict. When you detach, you stop internalizing their attacks. You stop questioning your worth and your parenting. Instead, you become grounded in your own sense of self-worth and confidence as a parent.

A Call to Action: Reclaim Your Power for the Sake of Your Children

Your children need you to be strong, stable, and emotionally present. They need a parent who can provide them with the security and love that only comes from a place of emotional strength. The narcissist in your life will continue to push your buttons and provoke you. But you don't have to let them control your emotions anymore.

Over the next 60 days, the E.M.P.O.W.E.R. System will guide you toward emotional freedom. This isn't just about co-parenting—it's about reclaiming your life. It's about breaking free from the grip of narcissistic manipulation and creating a future where you and your children thrive.

It won't be easy, but the results will be life-changing. By committing to the process, you'll not only protect yourself from further emotional harm, but you'll also model resilience and strength for your children. They'll see you standing firm, not reacting to the narcissist's provocations, and they'll learn from your example. You'll show them that no one has the power to control their emotions except themselves.

Are you ready to begin? Are you ready to reclaim your power and create a peaceful, empowering environment for you and your children?

The journey starts now.

Part 1: Reclaim Control

"You cannot control the behavior of others, but you can always choose how you respond to it." — Roy T. Bennett

In a world dominated by the chaos of co-parenting with a narcissist, the desire for control can feel elusive. It is not about controlling your ex-partner or even trying to manipulate the situation. It's about reclaiming control over your emotions, your reactions, and ultimately, your peace of mind. This chapter will guide you through the emotional landscape that narcissists create, showing you how to detach and regain power—not over them, but over yourself. The journey ahead will not be about winning battles but about stepping out of the war altogether.

Narcissists thrive on conflict. It's their lifeblood. To keep you emotionally entangled, they will stir up drama, twist narratives, and trigger your deepest fears. You, on the other hand, have likely been drawn into this battle more times than you can count—arguing, defending, and justifying yourself, only to realize nothing ever changes. In this emotional tug of war, the only way to regain your footing is to let go of the rope. Detachment is not about giving up; it's about freeing yourself from their control over your emotions.

Reclaiming control starts by understanding the emotional trap. Narcissists know how to manipulate situations to make you feel responsible for their behavior or the outcome of interactions. You may feel like you have to respond to every accusation or that your silence is a sign of weakness. This couldn't be further from the truth. True control lies in choosing how you respond.

Chapter 1

The Emotional Trap: Why Narcissists Thrive on Conflict

"Narcissists don't engage in conversation; they engage in conflict." — Dr. Ramani Durvasula

Narcissists and the Power of Conflict

Narcissists are not just drawn to conflict; they create it. They rely on it as a primary means of maintaining control over others. For them, conflict is more than a disagreement or misunderstanding—it is a tool to manipulate, destabilize, and assert dominance. By creating chaos, narcissists can keep their victims emotionally off-balance, ensuring they remain entangled in the narcissist's web of control.

Conflict as Fuel for Narcissistic Supply

Narcissists feed on what psychologists call "narcissistic supply"—the emotional reactions, attention, and energy they draw from others. Conflict is one of the easiest ways for them to generate this supply. When they provoke anger, frustration, or sadness in their victims, they gain power by dictating the emotional atmosphere of the relationship. This supply validates their sense of superiority and control.

For example, in a co-parenting situation, a narcissist might deliberately undermine a decision about the children, knowing it will provoke an emotional response from the other parent. By drawing their co-parent into a heated argument, they reaffirm their ability to control not just the conversation but the emotional state of the other person. The more emotional energy they extract, the more they feel validated in their dominance.

Creating Chaos to Shift Blame

One reason narcissists thrive on conflict is that it allows them to shift blame and deflect responsibility. By constantly stirring up disputes, they can position themselves as victims of unreasonable behavior, even though they are the ones instigating the turmoil. This tactic, often called gaslighting, causes their victims to question their own reality, making them more vulnerable to the narcissist's manipulations.

Consider a situation where a narcissist accuses their ex-partner of being "too emotional" or "unreasonable" during a conflict they themselves provoked. This classic reversal of roles keeps the narcissist in control, as their victim becomes preoccupied with defending themselves rather than recognizing the narcissist's role in creating the conflict.

Prolonging Emotional Engagement

Another way narcissists use conflict is by ensuring it is never fully resolved. While most people enter conflicts with the intention of finding a solution, narcissists do the opposite. They intentionally leave issues unresolved to keep the emotional engagement going. Each new disagreement, argument, or misunderstanding becomes an opportunity to pull their victim back into a cycle of emotional turmoil.

In this sense, conflict becomes a trap. Victims of narcissistic abuse often find themselves revisiting the same arguments over and over without ever reaching a resolution. The goal is not to fix the problem but to keep their victims emotionally entangled, ensuring the narcissist's control remains unchallenged.

Escalation as a Control Tactic

When a narcissist senses they are losing control, they often escalate conflicts to regain power. This might involve increasing the intensity of their provocations or making more extreme accusations. The escalation forces their victim to respond, usually with heightened emotions, thus feeding the narcissist's need for validation.

For instance, in the context of co-parenting, a narcissist might make outlandish claims about their ex-partner's parenting abilities, knowing this will provoke a defensive and emotional reaction. The more intense the conflict becomes, the more control the narcissist exerts, keeping their victim on the defensive.

Why Detachment is Key to Regaining Power

The power of detachment cannot be overstated when it comes to dealing with a narcissist. Emotional detachment means refusing to engage in the conflict they are trying to provoke. This doesn't mean giving up or being passive—it's about taking back control by deciding when and how you respond. The narcissist thrives on your emotional reactions; without them, they lose their grip.

Detachment lets you step back from the emotional rollercoaster they've put you on. When you detach, you stop feeding the cycle of conflict that fuels their need for control. It's a form of empowerment that allows you to protect your emotional well-being while safeguarding your children from the emotional fallout of their toxic tactics.

Detaching can be challenging, especially when the narcissist is using every tool in their arsenal to provoke a response. But as you build this skill, you'll notice a shift in your interactions over time. The narcissist will have less and less power over your emotional state, and their attempts to engage in conflict will lose their effectiveness. In this sense, detachment is not surrender but the act of reclaiming your power.

The Emotional Struggle of Letting Go

Detaching from conflict with a narcissistic co-parent is no easy feat. The emotional struggle is real, and validating those feelings is important. Many parents feel guilty when they start to pull away from the conflict. After all, society tells us that we should try to maintain a civil co-parenting relationship for the sake of the children. But when one parent is a narcissist, this becomes nearly impossible. The reality is that maintaining emotional distance from the narcissist is the healthiest option for both you and your children.

Guilt is often tied to the belief that not engaging in conflict means you're not doing enough to fix the situation. This is a myth that needs to be dispelled. Engaging in conflict only gives the narcissist more opportunities to manipulate and control. By detaching, you are setting boundaries that protect your emotional and mental health, allowing you to be a more present and stable parent for your children.

Validating Your Experience: You Are Not Alone

One of the most isolating aspects of co-parenting with a narcissist is the feeling that no one truly understands what you're going through. Narcissists are experts at presenting a polished image to the outside world, often making you appear as the problematic or unreasonable parent. This creates a cycle where you begin to doubt your own reality, questioning whether the narcissist really is as toxic as you feel they are.

It's important to acknowledge that your experiences are valid. The emotional abuse, the manipulations, the constant needling—these are all common tactics used by narcissists to keep their ex-partners in a state of confusion and emotional distress. Recognizing these behaviors for what they are is the first step in breaking free from the emotional trap.

You are not alone in this experience. Many parents have walked the same path and successfully navigated the complexities of co-parenting with a narcissist. Their stories show that it's possible to rise above the conflict and reclaim your peace of mind. By sharing real-life examples and offering actionable strategies, this book aims to provide the tools you need to detach, heal, and ultimately thrive despite the ongoing conflict.

Practical Steps to Achieve Detachment

1. **Set firm boundaries:** Clearly define what you will and will not tolerate in your interactions with the narcissist. This might include refusing to engage in arguments or limiting communication to written formats.

2. **Practice emotional neutrality:** The narcissist will attempt to bait you into conflict. Practice responding calmly and without emotional investment. Over time, this will reduce their power to control the situation.

3. **Create distance:** Both emotional and physical distance can be powerful tools in detachment. Whenever possible, limit face-to-face interactions and use written communication for co-parenting logistics.

4. **Focus on your own well-being:** Prioritize self-care and surround yourself with a support network that understands your situation. The stronger you are emotionally, the less vulnerable you will be to the narcissist's tactics.

5. **Remember the long game:** Detachment doesn't produce immediate results, and the narcissist may escalate their attempts to provoke you. Stay focused on your long-term emotional freedom and the well-being of your children.

Case Study: Detaching from Conflict to Reclaim Control in Co-Parenting with a Narcissist

Emily had been co-parenting her two children with her ex-husband, Mark, for three years after their divorce. Mark displayed classic narcissistic traits—constantly creating conflict, gaslighting Emily, and manipulating situations to appear as the reasonable parent while pushing Emily to emotional outbursts. He frequently used the children as pawns, causing confusion and distress in their lives. Every interaction, whether in person or via text, felt like a trap where Mark would provoke an emotional response from Emily. The ongoing conflict was exhausting and impacted her well-being and her ability to parent effectively.

Challenge: Emily was emotionally overwhelmed and found herself reacting to Mark's provocations, which led to frequent arguments. She felt guilty for not being able to maintain a peaceful co-parenting relationship and was afraid that by disengaging, she would be accused of being an unfit parent. Her primary concern was her children's well-being. Still, she didn't know how to protect them from the emotional fallout of Mark's behavior while detaching herself from the constant conflict.

Solution: Implement *Emotional Detachment*: After seeking therapy, Emily was introduced to the concept of emotional detachment. Her therapist explained that Mark's need for conflict was a form of control, and the only way to stop the cycle was to refuse to engage emotionally. Emily began by setting clear boundaries around communication. She moved all co-parenting discussions to written communication via email, limiting direct interaction. This gave her time to process Mark's inflammatory messages without reacting impulsively.

She also adopted the *Gray Rock Method*, responding to Mark's provocations with brief, neutral answers. The Gray Rock Method is a well-known technique in dealing with narcissists. The premise is simple: when you present yourself as emotionally unresponsive and uninteresting—like a gray rock—the narcissist loses interest in engaging with you. They thrive on drama; they are forced to seek it elsewhere if you don't provide any. When Mark attempted to escalate conflicts during exchanges of the children, Emily remained calm, refusing to engage. In situations where conflict seemed unavoidable, she shifted her focus to her children's needs rather than getting drawn into Mark's manipulations.

Emily also began to prioritize self-care and leaned on her support system. She joined a group for parents dealing with high-conflict ex-partners, where she found validation and emotional strength. As she detached emotionally, she discovered that Mark's provocations had less impact on her, and her emotional stability improved significantly.

Outcome: Over time, Emily noticed a significant reduction in the frequency and intensity of conflicts. Mark continued to attempt manipulation, but his lack of emotional fuel from Emily weakened his control. By focusing on her well-being and maintaining boundaries, Emily could parent from a place of peace and emotional stability, which positively impacted her children. They, too, became less anxious as the conflict between their parents decreased.

The most profound result was Emily's realization that she was not at all abandoning her responsibilities as a parent by detaching. Instead, she was reclaiming her emotional power and creating a healthier environment for her children.

Key Takeaways from Emily's Case

- **Boundaries are essential:** Moving communication to email and limiting face-to-face interaction gave Emily the space to process Mark's manipulations without reacting emotionally.

- **The Gray Rock Method works**: Responding in neutral, non-engaging ways reduced Mark's ability to provoke Emily and create conflict.

- **Support systems matter:** Finding a group of people who understood her challenges helped Emily stay strong and committed to emotional detachment.

- **Focus on children's well-being:** Detachment allowed Emily to parent from a place of peace, ultimately benefiting her children and reducing their exposure to conflict.

This case study illustrates the power of emotional detachment and how reclaiming control is possible even when co-parenting with a narcissist.

Chapter Wrap-Up

Narcissists thrive on conflict because it gives them a sense of control and power over others. By understanding this dynamic, you can start to detach from the cycle of manipulation and regain control over your emotions. This chapter has explored the tactics narcissists use to trap you in conflict, the importance of detachment as a strategy for empowerment, and the emotional challenges you may face along the way.

In this chapter, we explored the following key points:

- **Narcissists use conflict as a control tactic:** Conflict is not incidental but a deliberate strategy employed by narcissists to maintain emotional control over their ex-partners. By constantly provoking and engaging in disputes, they keep their victims emotionally invested and off balance.

- **Detachment is the key to regaining power:** Emotional detachment is an essential tool in breaking free from the narcissist's control. By refusing to react emotionally, you can reclaim your power and stop feeding the cycle of conflict.

- **Understanding the emotional struggle:** Letting go of conflict is difficult, and many feel guilt or doubt when detaching. However, reframing detachment as an act of self-protection and empowerment for both yourself and your children is crucial.

- **Practical steps to achieve detachment:** Strategies like setting boundaries, practicing emotional neutrality, and focusing on self-care are essential in minimizing the narcissist's ability to provoke conflict.

- **Validating your experience:** Narcissists often gaslight their victims, making them doubt their reality and feel isolated. Acknowledging and validating your feelings is the first step toward healing and reclaiming control.

As you begin to implement these strategies, you'll find that the narcissist's control weakens, and your sense of self strengthens. Remember, detachment isn't about giving up—it's about reclaiming your peace and power.

In the next chapter, we will explore how the ongoing conflict with a narcissistic co-parent can affect your children's emotional well-being. You'll learn actionable strategies to protect them from emotional harm while still maintaining your own detachment. By focusing on your children's well-being, you'll take another crucial step toward creating a stable and nurturing environment that shields them from the chaos of narcissistic manipulation.

Chapter 2

Protecting Your Children's Emotional Well-Being

"Children who grow up feeling secure, loved, and nurtured will face the world with confidence." — Jane Nelson

Co-parenting with a narcissist can be a psychological battlefield for your children. Children caught in the middle of narcissistic dynamics often experience emotional confusion, self-doubt, and a struggle to understand their worth. As a parent, you want to protect your children from this harmful influence, but how do you shield them from emotional damage while also navigating the complexities of co-parenting? Learning how to detach emotionally and create a stable, nurturing environment where your children can thrive despite the challenges is the answer.

In this chapter, we will look at the psychological impact of co-parenting with a narcissist on children and the crucial role emotional detachment plays in safeguarding their well-being. We'll provide actionable strategies that will help you protect your children not only from the immediate harm of a toxic co-parent but also from long-term emotional damage. By focusing on their needs, you will learn how to foster resilience and strength in your children, ensuring that they grow up in an emotionally healthy space.

Understanding the Psychological Impact on Children

When children grow up in an environment shaped by a narcissistic parent, their emotional and psychological development can be severely affected. Narcissists often engage in behaviors such as manipulation, gaslighting, and using children as pawns in their emotional games. These behaviors can leave children feeling emotionally isolated, confused, and conflicted about their self-worth.

Children raised in these environments might develop issues such as:

- **Low self-esteem:** Constant manipulation and emotional invalidation can lead children to believe they are not good enough.

- **Anxiety and confusion:** The unpredictability of a narcissistic parent's behavior often leads to children walking on eggshells, unsure of what to expect.

- **Emotional dysregulation:** Witnessing frequent emotional outbursts or silent treatments can disrupt a child's ability to manage their emotions healthily.

- **Difficulty trusting others:** Narcissists often undermine the child's ability to form stable relationships, teaching them that love is conditional and can be withdrawn at any moment.

The long-term psychological effects can include depression, anxiety disorders, and a propensity to form unhealthy relationships in adulthood. As parents co-parenting with a narcissist, it's crucial to recognize these warning signs early and intervene with strategies that prioritize the emotional well-being of your children.

Detachment: The Essential Tool for Protection

One of the most effective ways to shield your children from a narcissist's influence is by practicing emotional detachment from your ex. By doing so, you prevent the narcissist from having control over your emotional responses, allowing you to create a stable and calm environment for your children.

Here are the steps to successfully implement emotional detachment:

1. **Recognize the Narcissist's Tactics:** Understand that narcissists often thrive on eliciting emotional reactions. They might try to provoke you into arguments or manipulate situations to appear as the victim. Recognizing these tactics is the first step toward detaching emotionally. Don't allow their behavior to pull you into unnecessary confrontations.

2. **Shift Your Focus to Your Children:** Instead of getting caught up in the narcissist's games, make your children the center of your focus. Ask yourself, "What do my children need right now?" This shift in perspective will help you manage situations with greater

calm and clarity. Your children need stability, emotional support, and consistent love from you.

3. **Establish Clear Boundaries:** Set firm boundaries with your co-parent, especially regarding communication and decision-making about the children. Stick to agreed-upon plans and do not engage in discussions that deviate from parenting topics. Narcissists often use co-parenting to maintain control, so establishing clear limits is essential.

4. **Create Emotional Distance:** Practice responding to the narcissist in a calm, non-reactive manner. Narcissists will try to provoke emotional responses to maintain power in the relationship. Emotional distance ensures that their tactics don't destabilize your mental health, and it teaches your children that conflict can be managed with grace and calmness.

5. **Focus on What You Can Control:** You cannot change your narcissistic co-parent's behavior, but you can control how you respond to it. Keep your reactions measured and focus on creating a positive environment for your children when they are with you. Your emotional stability will serve as a buffer for them against the volatility of the other parent.

Actionable Strategies for Shielding Children

While detachment is a critical part of protecting your children, there are additional strategies you can use to shield them from further emotional harm:

- **Provide Consistency:** Children need structure and predictability to feel safe. Establish routines that give them a sense of stability, especially when they move between households. Knowing they can rely on consistent bedtime, meals, and activities can help reduce anxiety caused by a chaotic environment.

- **Validate Their Feelings:** Encourage open communication with your children. Let them express their emotions without fear of judgment or punishment. Narcissistic parents often dismiss or invalidate their children's feelings, so you must counterbalance this by validating and affirming their emotions.

- **Teach Emotional Resilience:** Equip your children with tools to navigate their emotions. Teach them mindfulness techniques or journaling exercises to help them process their feelings in a healthy way. Help them understand that while they can't control their narcissistic parent's behavior, they can control how they respond to it.

- **Encourage Healthy Relationships:** Surround your children with positive role models who can offer support and demonstrate healthy relationship dynamics. These relationships will show your children that love and trust don't need to come with manipulation or conditions.

- **Protect Their Self-Esteem:** Reinforce your children's strengths and talents. Help them build a strong sense of self-worth by celebrating their achievements, no matter how small. This counteracts the narcissist's attempts to undermine their confidence.

The Power of Detachment in Creating a Nurturing Environment

Detachment allows you to separate the toxicity of the narcissist from the emotional well-being of your children. By staying calm and centered, you can create a home environment that is emotionally safe, nurturing, and supportive. In this space, your children can grow without the fear of emotional manipulation or instability. Your example will teach them how to navigate difficult relationships without losing themselves.

A nurturing environment is not about shielding your children from every negative experience—this would be impossible in a co-parenting situation with a narcissist. Instead, it's about giving them the tools to navigate these challenges with emotional resilience and self-confidence. By practicing detachment and focusing on your children's needs, you are actively creating a buffer that protects them from long-term emotional harm.

Case Study: Emotional Detachment in Action – Protecting Children from a Narcissistic Co-Parent

Mike, a 38-year-old father of two, has been co-parenting with his ex-wife, Sarah, for five years. Sarah exhibits strong narcissistic traits—she's manipulative, controlling, and frequently uses their children, Ella (8) and Liam (11), as emotional pawns to provoke reactions from Mike. The constant conflicts have taken a toll on Mike's emotional well-being and have started affecting his children, who have shown signs of anxiety and confusion about their mother's erratic behavior.

Mike's goal is to protect his children from emotional harm while minimizing his own stress in dealing with Sarah. After much research, he decides to implement emotional detachment strategies and parallel parenting to shield the children from Sarah's toxic influence.

Step 1: Identifying Triggers

Situation: Sarah frequently manipulates the children into believing Mike is the cause of their problems. She cancels visits at the last minute and blames Mike for "interfering" in her parenting, often in front of Ella and Liam. This leads to confusion and resentment in the children toward Mike.

Trigger: Mike often felt compelled to defend himself when Sarah made these accusations, leading to heated arguments in front of the children. This created more tension and instability.

Detachment Strategy: Mike started recognizing that Sarah's behavior was designed to provoke a response and maintain control. He decided to stop engaging emotionally with her and focus on maintaining a calm demeanor, especially in front of the children. Instead of defending himself, Mike responded to Sarah's accusations with calm, neutral statements like, "I will only discuss matters related to the children. Let's stick to our agreed-upon parenting plan."

Step 2: Setting Boundaries

Situation: Sarah often called Mike late at night to discuss non-urgent issues, using these calls to continue arguments that had nothing to do with the children. This would disrupt Mike's personal time and make him feel constantly on edge.

Boundary: Mike established a clear boundary: all communication with Sarah would take place in writing through a co-parenting app, and only urgent matters related to the children's health or safety would be discussed over the phone. He communicated this boundary calmly but firmly to Sarah, stating, "Please use the app for all non-urgent communication. I will only respond to calls if there is an emergency regarding Ella or Liam."

Outcome: Although Sarah initially resisted and tried to provoke Mike further by sending accusatory messages in the app, Mike stuck to this boundary. Mike reduced his stress by refusing to engage in emotional discussions and protected his personal time.

Step 3: Creating Emotional Stability for the Children

Situation: Ella and Liam were often confused about their mother's unpredictable behavior. On some visits, she would shower them with affection; on others, she would be distant or critical, leaving the children feeling insecure.

Detachment and Routine: Mike focused on creating a consistent, nurturing environment when the children were with him. He established clear routines for bedtime, homework, and family activities so that Ella and Liam knew what to expect in his home. During his time with them, Mike provided reassurance by encouraging open conversations about their feelings and validating their emotions. He reminded them, "You can feel however you feel, and you can always talk to me about it."

Affirmation Practice: Mike encouraged Ella and Liam to practice daily affirmations to boost their self-esteem. Each morning, they would repeat phrases like, "I am strong, I am loved, and I am important." This practice helped the children build emotional resilience, even when their father's behavior was unpredictable.

Step 4: Managing Emotional Manipulation

Situation: On one occasion, Sarah told Liam that Mike was "trying to keep them apart," blaming him for a visitation schedule change caused by her own last-minute cancellation. Liam returned to Mike's house upset and angry, accusing him of controlling the situation.

Mike's Response: Instead of getting defensive, Mike calmly explained the facts to Liam, saying, "I'm sorry you're upset, and it's okay to feel that way. The schedule changed because your mother had to cancel, not because I wanted to. I would never stop you from seeing her." He then validated Liam's feelings by acknowledging how difficult it must be for him when plans change unexpectedly.

By staying emotionally neutral, Mike helped Liam see the situation clearly without feeling like he had to choose sides. This also prevented the conflict from escalating further.

Results: A Shift in Emotional Dynamics

Over the next few months, Mike noticed several positive changes in both his own emotional well-being and the children's behavior:

- **Personal Well-being:** Mike felt less stressed and more in control of his emotions. By practicing detachment, he no longer allowed Sarah's provocations to dictate his mood. This gave him more energy and mental space to focus on his children.

- **Children's Emotional Health:** Ella and Liam began showing more emotional stability. While they still struggled with some of their mother's behaviors, they had fewer emotional outbursts and expressed their feelings more openly with Mike. The routines and emotional validation at Mike's home gave them a sense of security and predictability.

- **Reduction in Conflict:** The shift to written communication through the co-parenting app significantly reduced the number of conflicts between Sarah and Mike. By sticking to his boundaries and refusing to engage in emotional arguments, Mike minimized opportunities for Sarah to manipulate him.

- **Improved Relationships:** The children began to trust Mike more as they saw him consistently respond calmly, even when their mother attempted to stir conflict. They felt safe talking to him about their emotions, and Mike's focus on emotional resilience helped them cope better with their mother's erratic behavior.

Mike's case illustrates how practicing emotional detachment, setting clear boundaries, and creating a nurturing environment can protect children from the harmful effects of co-parenting with a narcissist. By shifting his focus away from Sarah's manipulations and toward the children's emotional well-being, Mike was able to reduce conflict and provide a stable, loving space where her children could thrive.

Parents in similar situations can follow Mike's lead by recognizing narcissistic behavior, practicing emotional detachment, and focusing on fostering emotional resilience in their children. Although co-parenting with a narcissist is never easy, these strategies offer a path toward peace and stability for both parents and children.

Chapter Wrap-Up

In this chapter, we discussed the psychological impact of co-parenting with a narcissist and the essential role of emotional detachment in protecting your children from harm. Narcissistic behavior can have long-lasting effects on children's self-esteem, emotional development, and mental health, but there are effective strategies you can use to shield them.

Key strategies include:

- **Emotional Detachment:** Learning to recognize the narcissist's manipulative tactics and responding calmly and neutrally.

- **Setting Boundaries:** Establishing clear, non-negotiable limits in your communication and interactions with the narcissistic co-parent.

- **Focusing on Children's Well-being:** Shifting your focus away from the narcissist's provocations and toward creating a stable, nurturing environment for your children.

- **Teaching Emotional Resilience:** Helping your children develop the emotional intelligence and resilience needed to navigate their relationship with a narcissistic parent.

Through detachment, boundary-setting, and nurturing your children's emotional health, you can reduce the impact of narcissistic manipulation and foster a safe, supportive environment where your children can thrive. These strategies protect your children's emotional well-being and empower you to regain control of your own emotional landscape.

In the next chapter, we'll explore the importance of prioritizing your mental health as a parent. You cannot pour from an empty cup, and protecting your emotional well-being is vital to remaining strong and steady for your children. We'll dive into practical self-care strategies, ways to manage stress, and how to reclaim your emotional power from the narcissistic co-parent. Taking care of yourself is just as important as taking care of your children, and in this chapter, you'll learn how to do both effectively.

Chapter 3

The Guilt of Letting Go: Overcoming Emotional Attachments

"Guilt is the thief of life."— Anthony Hopkins

In the midst of family conflict, many parents find themselves overwhelmed by the emotional burden of guilt, fear, and attachment. The idea of detaching from these situations can seem impossible, as though it means abandoning their role as a protector or caregiver. Yet, the opposite is true: learning to let go is not an act of weakness; it is a conscious, deliberate decision to protect both your emotional well-being and that of your children. In this chapter, we will explore the complexities of emotional detachment, address the common misconceptions surrounding it, and offer mindset shifts to help you navigate the guilt that often accompanies this process.

Letting go doesn't mean you are walking away from your responsibilities. On the contrary, it is essential to create a healthier emotional environment for yourself and your family. Many parents, especially in high-conflict situations, mistakenly believe staying engaged in these conflicts shows strength. However, knowing when to step back and allow yourself the emotional distance necessary to foster healing and growth is the real strength. Detaching does not mean you no longer care; it means you care enough to protect both yourself and your children from the toxic cycle of conflict.

Recognizing the Emotional Triggers Behind Guilt

One of the most significant challenges parents face in emotionally detaching from conflict is the overwhelming guilt that comes with it. This guilt often stems from deep-rooted beliefs about what it means to be a "good" parent. We are conditioned to believe that a good parent is always present, always engaged, and always solving problems for their children. When we step back, even for a moment, that conditioning makes us feel like we are failing our duties.

Understanding that this guilt is not based on reality but on societal expectations that may no longer serve you or your family is crucial. To begin the process of detachment, you must first identify where your guilt is coming from. Are you afraid that stepping back will make you look like a bad parent? Do you fear that detachment means abandonment? These are common emotional triggers that need to be addressed so that you can move forward.

Reframing Emotional Detachment as Strength

Emotional detachment is often misunderstood as indifference or coldness. However, detachment is not about cutting off your emotions entirely; it's about setting boundaries that protect your emotional health. Reframing detachment as a positive act of strength is a critical mindset shift that will help you overcome the guilt associated with it.

Start by recognizing that staying emotionally entangled in conflict doesn't solve the problem—it perpetuates it. When you are constantly reactive, you're not in control of the situation. Detachment, on the other hand, allows you to respond thoughtfully rather than react impulsively. By stepping back, you are giving yourself the emotional clarity needed to approach problems with a calm, clear mind. This, in turn, creates a more stable and peaceful environment for your children, who are often caught in the crossfire of unresolved conflict.

Think of emotional detachment as putting on your oxygen mask first. Just as flight attendants remind us that we must secure our own oxygen before assisting others, emotional detachment ensures that you are in the best possible emotional state to support your children. It is not about abandoning them but showing them how to navigate conflict without becoming overwhelmed by it.

Steps to Overcome Guilt and Let Go

To begin the journey of emotional detachment, follow these actionable steps:

Acknowledge Your Guilt: The first step is to recognize and acknowledge the guilt you feel. Write down your thoughts and identify the specific beliefs causing your guilt..

Challenge Your Beliefs: Ask yourself whether these beliefs are serving you or your family. Are they based on reality or rooted in societal expectations that no longer align with your current situation?

Reframe Detachment as Strength: Remind yourself that emotional detachment is not a sign of weakness. It is an act of strength that allows you to protect yourself and your children from unnecessary conflict.

Set Clear Boundaries: Establish boundaries that protect your emotional well-being. This might mean limiting your interactions with certain individuals or choosing not to engage in every argument.

Focus on What You Can Control: Let go of the need to control everything and focus on what you can control—your reactions, emotions, and mental health.

Seek Support: Don't be afraid to seek support from a therapist or a support group. Having a neutral third party can help you gain perspective and offer strategies for emotional detachment.

The Impact on Your Children

One of the most significant benefits of emotional detachment is its positive impact on your children. When you let go of the guilt and conflict, you create a more stable and peaceful environment for them. Children are incredibly perceptive and can pick up on the emotional energy in their surroundings. By detaching from conflict, you teach them that it's okay to set boundaries and prioritize their emotional health.

In many cases, children of parents who have learned to detach report feeling less stressed and more secure emotionally. They no longer feel like they are caught in the middle of their parents' battles. Instead, they see their parents as calm, composed individuals who handle conflict with grace and maturity.

Case Study: Amber's Journey to Emotional Detachment

Amber, a 40-year-old mother of two, had been separated from her husband, Mark, for three years. Despite the separation, Amber found herself constantly engaged in emotional conflicts with Mark over their children. Every decision - whether about school, extracurricular activities, or custody schedules turned into a prolonged argument. Amber felt a deep sense of guilt whenever she thought about detaching from these conflicts, fearing that it would make her appear uncaring or dismissive of her children's needs.

Amber's guilt was rooted in her belief that, as a mother, she had to be involved in every decision, every argument, and every moment of her children's lives. The thought of stepping back felt like abandonment. However, this constant emotional involvement was taking a toll on her mental health, leaving her exhausted and emotionally drained. Her children, witnessing the ongoing tension between their parents, began showing signs of stress—anxiety, difficulty concentrating in school, and emotional outbursts at home.

Challenge: Amber realized that her approach was unsustainable. She was emotionally overwhelmed, and it was affecting her ability to meaningfully be present for her children. At the same time, she couldn't shake the guilt that came with the idea of detaching from the conflict with Mark. She needed a way to let go without feeling like she was failing her children.

Mindset Shift: After attending a parenting workshop on co-parenting and emotional boundaries, Amber was introduced to the concept of emotional detachment as a form of protection—not only for herself but for her children. The workshop highlighted research showing that children benefit from seeing their parents manage conflict in a healthy way and that ongoing exposure to parental conflict can lead to anxiety, depression, and behavioral issues.

This new perspective was a revelation for Amber. She began to see emotional detachment not as abandonment but as a necessary step to protect her children from the harmful effects of constant conflict. By setting boundaries, Amber could model healthier conflict resolution for her children, showing them that it was possible to navigate difficult situations without becoming emotionally overwhelmed.

Implementation: Amber started by setting clear boundaries with Mark. She decided that unless the conversation was directly about the children's immediate needs, she would not engage in drawn-out arguments. She learned to recognize when the conversation was escalating into conflict and would calmly remove herself from the situation. Additionally, Amber practiced mindfulness techniques, like deep breathing and taking breaks, to manage her emotions during stressful interactions.

To reinforce this new approach, Amber also communicated with her children in an age-appropriate way. She explained that while she and their father might not always agree, they were both working to create a more peaceful environment. She reassured them that her detachment from conflict didn't mean she cared any less for them; it simply meant she wanted to protect them from unnecessary stress.

Results: Within a few months, Amber noticed significant changes. She felt more in control of her emotions and less guilty about not engaging in every argument. Her children, who had previously shown signs of emotional distress, became more relaxed. The atmosphere at home improved, and Amber found that she could enjoy her time with her children without the shadow of conflict hanging over them.

Perhaps most significantly, her relationship with Mark also became less combative. By refusing to engage in emotional arguments, Amber shifted the dynamic between them. The communication became more focused on the practicalities of co-parenting, and the hostile emotional undertones that once characterized their interactions began to fade.

Key Takeaways:

- **Emotional detachment is not abandonment:** Amber's case illustrates that detaching emotionally from conflict doesn't mean you are neglecting your children. It can be an act of strength and protection, creating a healthier environment for both the parent and the child.

- **Setting boundaries is essential:** Amber's success was largely due to her ability to set clear boundaries with her ex-husband. By refusing to engage in every argument, she was able to reduce the emotional burden on herself and her children.

- **Children benefit from emotional clarity:** When parents detach from conflict, children experience less stress and anxiety. Amber's children felt more secure and relaxed when they saw their mother modeling healthier emotional behavior.

Amber's story provides a real-world example of how emotional detachment can transform the parent's emotional well-being and the overall family dynamic. It underscores the power of letting go to protect oneself and one's children from the toxic effects of ongoing conflict.

Chapter Wrap-Up

In this chapter, we explored the complex emotions that parents face when considering emotional detachment, particularly the guilt that often accompanies the decision to step back from conflict. We reframed emotional detachment as an act of strength rather than abandonment, helping parents realize that letting go of unnecessary emotional involvement protects both themselves and their children.

Key insights included identifying the triggers that cause guilt, challenging the belief that staying engaged in conflict is the only way to show love, and understanding how setting healthy boundaries can lead to a more peaceful family environment. We also looked at real-life examples of parents who successfully detached from conflict and experienced positive outcomes for themselves and their children.

The next section of this book introduces the ***E.M.P.O.W.E.R. System,*** the core framework that will guide you toward emotional freedom and co-parenting mastery. This system is specifically designed to help you navigate the complex challenges of co-parenting with a narcissist, empowering you to reclaim control over your emotions, mindset, and interactions.

Part II: Mastering Emotional Freedom

"The only person you are destined to become is the person you decide to be." — *Ralph Waldo Emerson*

For parents co-parenting with a narcissistic ex-partner, the emotional toll is exhausting. Every interaction feels like a manipulation, a trap designed to provoke a reaction, which keeps them tethered to conflict. Yet, emotional freedom is not just a distant goal but a practical, achievable shift in how one responds to these provocations. The E.M.P.O.W.E.R. System will teach you to regulate your emotions, detach from conflict without stepping away from your parental responsibilities, and regain your emotional autonomy.

In this section of the book, you will learn that mastering emotional freedom is the foundation of reclaiming your life and protecting your children. It's about building emotional resilience, adopting an empowered mindset, and developing practical daily habits that foster strength and clarity. Every step you take to master emotional freedom breaks the cycle of manipulation, allowing you to create a safe, stable environment for yourself and your children.

Chapter 4

The E.M.P.O.W.E.R. System: Your Path to Co-Parenting Mastery

"Feelings are much like waves; we can't stop them from coming, but we can choose which ones to surf." – Jonatan Mårtensson

In the world of co-parenting with a narcissistic ex-partner, emotional detachment may seem like a distant dream. However, the E.M.PO.W.E.R. System framework is specifically designed to guide you through that journey, turning emotional overwhelm into resilience and empowering you to regain control of your life. This chapter is your roadmap to breaking free from emotional cycles, setting the foundation for a healthier co-parenting relationship, and ultimately reclaiming your sense of peace.

As you read on, you'll discover that mastery over your emotions isn't just a lofty goal—it's the key to protecting yourself and your children from manipulation and unnecessary conflict.

Understanding the E.M.P.O.W.E.R. System Framework

The E.M.P.O.W.E.R. System framework is an actionable, step-by-step guide designed to help you reclaim control, maintain emotional balance, and foster a healthy co-parenting dynamic. It addresses the unique challenges you face in co-parenting with a narcissist and provides practical, effective strategies to overcome them.

The framework is structured around seven core components:

Emotions – Regulate emotional reactions to prevent your ex-partner from manipulating or provoking you.

Mindset – Shift from a victim mentality to one of empowerment and self-assurance.

Practices – Build consistent habits that reinforce emotional strength and clarity.

Obstacles – Identify and navigate the legal, financial, and emotional hurdles that often arise in co-parenting.

Withdrawal – Use techniques like the Gray Rock Method to emotionally disengage without neglecting your parenting responsibilities.

Enforcement – Develop and maintain boundaries with confidence, ensuring your ex-partner respects them.

Resilience – Cultivate long-term emotional resilience for both yourself and your children, creating an environment of stability and peace.

Each of these elements serves as a building block toward mastering emotional freedom and becoming an empowered co-parent.

Emotions: Regulating Your Reactions

When you're co-parenting with a narcissist, emotional provocation is a common tactic used to draw you into conflict. Your first challenge in the E.M.P.O.W.E.R. System framework is learning how to manage your emotional reactions. This isn't about suppressing your feelings but recognizing and regulating them to protect your mental and emotional well-being.

Narcissists thrive on chaos and the more emotional turmoil they can cause, the more power they feel they have. Understanding this dynamic is crucial because it allows you to step back and see their provocations for what they truly are—manipulative tools meant to control you.

The goal here is to practice emotional detachment. This doesn't mean you stop caring about your children or the co-parenting arrangement; instead, it's about not allowing the narcissist to control your emotional state. Techniques such as deep breathing, grounding exercises, and cognitive reframing can help you shift your focus from reacting emotionally to responding calmly and rationally.

Mindset: Shifting from Victim to Empowered Co-parent

The second step of the E.M.P.O.W.E.R. System framework focuses on reshaping your mindset. For many co-parents, it's easy to feel trapped in a cycle of conflict, helplessness, and victimhood. But adopting an empowerment mindset means recognizing that while you cannot control the narcissist's behavior, you can control how you respond to it.

This shift begins by reframing your thought patterns. Instead of viewing yourself as a victim of the narcissist's manipulations, start seeing yourself as someone in control of your emotional boundaries. This mindset shift is vital because it frees you from the emotional entanglement that narcissists rely on to maintain their influence over you.

Affirmations can play a key role in this transition. For example, reminding yourself, "I control my responses, not them," or "I am empowered to create a peaceful environment for my children," reinforces your sense of agency and helps you internalize this new perspective.

Practices: Building Daily Habits for Strength

A shift in mindset alone isn't enough—you need to back it up with consistent daily practices that reinforce your emotional strength. The E.M.P.O.W.E.R. System framework encourages developing habits that build mental fortitude, reduce stress, and keep you grounded, no matter how chaotic the co-parenting relationship becomes.

Start small. Incorporate practices like daily journaling, where you can reflect on your emotions, challenges, and progress. Mindfulness exercises can help you stay present and less reactive in triggering situations, while self-care routines ensure you're looking after your well-being.

Over time, these small habits will accumulate, creating a foundation of emotional strength that allows you to respond to provocations calmly rather than out of frustration or anger.

Obstacles: Navigating Legal, Financial, and Emotional Hurdles

Co-parenting with a narcissist isn't just emotionally taxing—it also comes with a host of logistical challenges. From navigating legal disputes to managing financial burdens, these obstacles can feel overwhelming. The key to overcoming these hurdles is preparation.

A major part of this preparation involves building a support network. Legal counsel, financial advisors, and therapists can all provide crucial guidance, helping you stay one step ahead. It's important to document everything—any legal agreements, communication with your ex-partner, and any behavioral patterns you observe. This documentation protects you legally and creates a sense of security, knowing that you have a solid plan in place to navigate potential obstacles.

Additionally, a strong support system of friends and family can offer emotional support and practical advice as you deal with these hurdles.

Withdrawal: Detaching Without Disengaging

Detachment doesn't mean disengagement. It's possible to emotionally withdraw from unnecessary conflict without abandoning your parenting responsibilities. One of the most effective strategies for this is the Gray Rock Method, or making yourself as uninteresting as possible to your ex-partner.

By refusing to react to their provocations and keeping your responses neutral and unemotional, you minimize the narcissist's ability to manipulate you. This form of detachment can significantly reduce conflict, but it requires consistency. Narcissists often escalate their tactics when they realize they are losing control, so it's essential to stay firm and continue practicing emotional detachment even when the pressure increases.

Enforcement: Maintaining Boundaries with Confidence

Boundaries are the cornerstone of a healthy co-parenting relationship. But maintaining those boundaries is often a challenge with a narcissist. The E.M.P.O.W.E.R. System framework emphasizes the importance of setting clear, non-negotiable boundaries and enforcing them consistently.

This can involve simple yet firm strategies, like limiting communication to specific topics and times or refusing to engage in arguments. When boundaries are violated, document the incidents and calmly but assertively remind your ex-partner of the agreed-upon limits.

Over time, this consistent boundary enforcement will help diminish the narcissist's ability to provoke conflict, allowing you to protect your peace and that of your children.

Resilience: Building Lasting Emotional Strength

Resilience is the final, yet most crucial, piece of the E.M.P.O.W.E.R. System framework. It's not enough to manage day-to-day interactions with a narcissist—you need to build long-term emotional strength that allows you to bounce back from setbacks and stay on course.

Resilience comes from consistent self-care, emotional regulation, and boundary enforcement but also requires a forward-thinking approach. Encourage your children to develop emotional resilience by teaching them coping mechanisms for dealing with their narcissistic parent. Over time, this resilience will create a stable and emotionally secure environment for your family, even in the face of challenges.

Chapter Wrap-up

This chapter sets the stage for a transformative journey, providing you with actionable steps to apply each framework element in your life. You were introduced to the E.M.P.O.W.E.R. System framework, a structured guide designed to help readers regain emotional control and establish a healthier co-parenting relationship. The framework consists of seven core components:

1. **Emotions** – Mastering emotional regulation to prevent manipulation from a narcissistic ex-partner.

2. **Mindset** – Shifting from a victim mentality to an empowered co-parenting perspective.

3. **Practices** – Establishing daily habits like journaling, mindfulness, and self-care to maintain emotional strength.

4. **Obstacles** – Overcoming legal, financial, and emotional hurdles through preparation and support systems.

5. **Withdrawal** – Using methods like the gray rock technique to emotionally detach from conflict while still being present as a parent.

6. **Enforcement** – Maintaining and enforcing firm boundaries with confidence and consistency.

7. **Resilience** – Building long-term emotional strength to create a stable environment for both parent and children.

By mastering the E.M.P.O.W.E.R. System framework, you can create an environment where you and your children can thrive, free from the emotional manipulation of a narcissistic ex-partner.

As you now understand the core components of the E.M.P.O.W.E.R. System framework, the next essential step is diving deeper into the first element—**Emotions**. Regulating your emotional responses is the foundation of your empowerment journey, and it sets the tone for all your future interactions with your narcissistic ex-partner. In the following chapter, you will discover practical techniques to recognize and manage your emotional triggers, allowing you to respond calmly rather than being drawn into conflict.

Chapter 5

Emotions: Regulating Your Reactions

"Your emotions are the slaves to your thoughts, and you are the slave to your emotions." – Elizabeth Gilbert

In moments of emotional intensity, it's easy to feel like the world is spinning out of control. Whether it's a sharp comment from an ex-partner, a heated argument, or an unexpected setback, emotional triggers can push us into reactions we later regret. The key to empowerment lies in recognizing these moments and choosing a calm, measured response instead of being driven by knee-jerk emotions. This chapter will guide you through the process of identifying emotional triggers and regulating your reactions in ways that give you back your power and control over your emotional landscape.

Emotions are a natural and healthy part of life, but when unchecked, they can lead us into destructive cycles—particularly when dealing with a manipulative ex-partner. By learning to regulate your emotional responses, you can reclaim your agency, ensuring you're no longer a puppet of your emotions or anyone else's provocations. Calm responses disarm those who seek to control you through manipulation, ultimately strengthening your emotional resilience and sense of self. Understanding how to manage these triggers is the first step toward emotional liberation and empowerment.

Recognizing Emotional Triggers

The first step to regulating your reactions is understanding what triggers emotional responses. These triggers often stem from past experiences, personal insecurities, or unhealed emotional wounds. They can be specific words, actions, or situations that remind you of unresolved feelings or past pain. When someone pushes a button—whether intentionally or not—our initial instinct is often defensive or reactive. But what if, instead of immediately reacting, you paused and recognized the trigger for what it was: a reflection of your past rather than your present?

Common Emotional Triggers:

- **Criticism** – Feeling attacked or undervalued when someone points out a flaw or shortcoming.

- **Rejection** – Experiencing a sense of abandonment, dismissal, or disapproval, leading to feelings of unworthiness.

- **Injustice** – A deep frustration when you perceive that something is unfair, unjust, or violates your personal values.

- **Failure** – The fear of not measuring up, making mistakes, or letting others down, which can trigger anxiety or shame.

- **Comparison** – Feeling inadequate or insecure when comparing yourself to others, leading to jealousy or self-doubt.

These triggers don't emerge from nowhere. They are often rooted in childhood experiences, past relationships, or core beliefs you've carried about yourself over time. By identifying these triggers, you can start to predict when and where they might appear. This awareness allows you to choose a response rather than reacting on autopilot.

Recognizing your emotional triggers is like turning on a light in a dark room—it allows you to see what you've been stumbling over and avoid it in the future. By bringing these triggers into your conscious awareness, you gain the power to control how you respond to them rather than being controlled by them.

Techniques for Managing Emotional Triggers

Once you've identified your emotional triggers, the next step is developing techniques to manage them. Emotional regulation is about training yourself to respond calmly, even when every fiber of your being wants to lash out or retreat in fear. It's not about suppressing emotions but finding healthy ways to process and respond to them.

- **Pause and Breathe:** One of the simplest yet most effective techniques is to take a deep breath before reacting. When you breathe deeply, you engage the parasympathetic nervous system, which calms your body and mind. This pause creates space between the trigger and your response, giving you time to think rather than act impulsively. In that brief pause, you can choose to respond from a place of calm rather than emotional reactivity.

- **Reframe the Situation**: After taking that pause, try reframing the situation. Ask yourself, "Is this really as bad as it seems?" or "What might this person be experiencing that made them act this way?" Often, our triggers magnify a situation beyond its actual scope. By shifting your perspective, you can reduce the intensity of your emotional reaction. For instance, instead of seeing criticism as a personal attack, you could view it as an opportunity for growth or improvement.

- **Practice Mindfulness:** Mindfulness is about staying present in the moment without judgment. When you practice mindfulness, you become more aware of your emotions as they arise rather than being swept away by them. This allows you to observe your feelings without immediately reacting, helping you stay grounded and more in control of your emotional state. Mindfulness exercises, such as focusing on your breath or doing a body scan, can help you stay connected to the present moment and reduce emotional overwhelm.

- **Set Emotional Boundaries:** It's also important to set boundaries - with others and yourself. If you know certain situations or conversations are likely to trigger you, you can proactively decide how to handle them. For example, you should limit contact with your manipulative ex or choose not to engage in certain discussions that are likely to escalate. Setting emotional boundaries helps protect your emotional well-being and proactively prevents you from being drawn into situations that undermine your peace of mind.

- **Cognitive Restructuring:** This technique challenges negative thought patterns contributing to emotional reactions. For example, when your ex-partner criticizes you, you might initially think, "They are always trying to make me feel small." Cognitive restructuring involves questioning that thought: Is this true? Are they trying to hurt me, or am I interpreting their behavior through a damaged filter? Why am I investing myself in their opinion of me? By challenging these thoughts, you can shift your emotional response.

The Power of Calm Responses

Remaining calm when someone is provoking you is one of the most powerful things you can do—not just for yourself but for the dynamic of the relationship. When you stay calm, it disempowers the other person's attempts to manipulate or control you. A manipulative ex-partner may rely on emotional outbursts, gaslighting, or passive-aggressive behavior to maintain control, but when you respond calmly, they lose their grip on the situation. Your emotional calmness acts as a shield, protecting you from being pulled into their emotional drama.

Why Calm Responses Work:

- **They shift the dynamic** – The person trying to provoke you doesn't get the reaction they're looking for, which can disarm and frustrate them.

- **They protect your mental health** – Instead of getting caught up in cycles of anger, frustration, or sadness, you maintain control over your emotional state, preserving your mental well-being.

- **They reinforce your boundaries** – When you respond calmly, you send a clear message that you will not be manipulated, drawn into conflict, or used as an emotional punching bag.

It's important to remember that calmness is not a sign of passivity or indifference. It's a conscious choice to protect your peace and preserve your emotional energy. When you refuse to be provoked, you shift the power balance, making it clear that you're in charge of your emotions, not the other person. Over time, this practice helps to solidify your emotional resilience and empowers you to handle any future provocations with grace.

Emotional Regulation as a Path to Empowerment

Learning to regulate your emotions isn't just about surviving difficult moments—it's about thriving in them. Emotional regulation leads to empowerment because it frees you from the tyranny of external forces. Instead of being reactive, you become proactive, deciding how to respond in a way that aligns with your values and long-term goals.

Empowerment through emotional regulation is about reclaiming your narrative. It's the difference between letting someone else's actions dictate your feelings and deciding for yourself how you want to feel. When you master emotional regulation, you understand that while you can't control how others behave, you can always control how you respond. This shift in perspective transforms your interactions and relationships, particularly when dealing with manipulative or toxic individuals.

Key Steps to Achieve Emotional Empowerment:

- **Acknowledge Your Emotions** – Don't ignore or downplay your feelings. Recognize them, name them, and understand where they come from.

- **Pause Before Responding** – Give yourself time to think before reacting. This prevents knee-jerk reactions and allows for more thoughtful responses.

- **Choose Your Response** – Decide how you want to respond based on what's best for you, not based on the trigger. This may mean walking away, setting a boundary, or addressing the situation calmly.

- **Reflect on the Outcome** – After the situation has passed, reflect on how you handled it and what you learned. Emotional regulation is a skill that improves with practice.

Building Emotional Resilience

Resilience is the ability to bounce back from difficult experiences, and emotional resilience is no different. By regulating your emotions, you build this resilience over time. Each time you successfully manage an emotional trigger, you strengthen your ability to handle future challenges more easily and confidently.

Why Emotional Resilience Matters:

- **It protects you from emotional exhaustion** – Constant emotional highs and lows can be draining. Resilience helps you maintain balance and conserve energy.

- **It allows you to grow** – Every emotional challenge becomes an opportunity to strengthen your emotional muscles and expand your capacity for handling future stressors.

- **It empowers you** – The more resilient you are, the less vulnerable you are to manipulation, emotional upheaval, and external pressures. You become the anchor in your own emotional storm.

Resilience doesn't mean you won't feel triggered or upset; it means you've developed the tools to handle those feelings in a healthy, constructive way. And with time, these tools become second nature, empowering you to face even the most challenging situations calmly and confidently.

Case Study: Maria's Overcoming Emotional Triggers and Reclaiming Power in a Toxic Relationship

Maria, a 38-year-old marketing executive, had recently gone through a difficult divorce from her husband of 12 years. The separation was emotionally taxing, and although the marriage had officially ended, her ex-husband continued to try and manipulate her emotionally. Every time they interacted—whether through co-parenting discussions or shared social circles—Maria was triggered by his critical comments and passive-aggressive behavior.

Maria noticed that after these encounters, she would spend hours or even days feeling angry, frustrated, and emotionally drained. She often reacted impulsively during conversations with her ex, saying things she later regretted, which only seemed to fuel his manipulative tactics. Maria realized she needed to regain control of her emotions to protect her mental health and stop allowing her ex-husband to have so much power over her.

Challenge: Maria's main challenge was learning how to regulate her emotional reactions during interactions with her ex-husband. His critical remarks and underhanded comments triggered deep feelings of inadequacy and anger, stemming from years of being emotionally undermined during the marriage. Whenever he said something negative about her parenting or life decisions, Maria reacted defensively, escalating the tension and leaving her feeling emotionally exhausted.

Maria wanted to:

- Identify and understand her emotional triggers.

- Develop strategies to respond calmly during provocations.

- Build emotional resilience so her ex-husband's manipulative tactics no longer affect her.

Solution: Maria began working on emotional regulation techniques, using many strategies discussed in this chapter.

1. **Identifying Emotional Triggers:** Maria's first step was identifying the triggers that set her off during interactions with her ex-husband. She realized that the main trigger was criticism, particularly when it involved her role as a mother. Her ex-husband would often make comments like, "You never think about what's best for the kids," or, "You've always been so selfish, and it's showing in your parenting." These comments struck at the heart of Maria's insecurities, leading to an immediate emotional reaction.

2. **Cognitive Restructuring:** To manage these triggers, Maria practiced cognitive restructuring. When her ex-husband made a critical remark, instead of reacting defensively, she began challenging the negative thoughts that immediately followed. For example, instead of thinking, "Maybe I really am a bad mother," she restructured the thought to, "This is his opinion, but it's not

true. I know I'm doing my best for my children." By reframing her thoughts, Maria reduced the emotional charge of the trigger.

3. **Practicing the Pause:** During conversations with her ex-husband, Maria implemented the "pause" technique. Whenever she felt the initial sting of his words, she took a deep breath and paused before responding. This brief moment of reflection allowed her to choose a more measured response rather than reacting impulsively. On several occasions, Maria opted not to respond at all, realizing that engaging in the argument would only escalate the situation.

4. **Boundary Setting:** Maria also set firm emotional boundaries. She communicated to her ex-husband that she would not engage in conversations that involved personal attacks or criticism of her parenting. "I'm willing to discuss decisions about the kids, but I won't engage in conversations that involve insults or personal attacks," she told him. If he crossed this boundary, Maria would calmly end the conversation by walking away or hanging up the phone.

5. **Mindfulness and Self-Soothing Techniques:** In moments when Maria felt emotionally overwhelmed, she practiced mindfulness by observing her feelings without judgment. She noted where in her body she felt the tension (usually in her chest and shoulders) and used deep breathing exercises to calm herself. She also visualized placing her emotions in a mental "container," which helped her create emotional distance and allowed her to process the situation without reacting emotionally.

6. **Emotional Reflection and Growth:** Maria kept a journal to reflect on her emotional reactions and the progress she made. After each interaction with her ex-husband, she would write about what triggered her, how she responded, and how she could improve. Over time, Maria noticed that her emotional triggers were losing their intensity. By reflecting on her experiences, she gradually built emotional resilience, making it easier to manage her emotions in future interactions.

Outcome: Within a few months of practicing emotional regulation techniques, Maria experienced significant improvements in her emotional well-being. Her ex-husband's manipulative comments no longer held the same power over her. While she still felt triggered at times, Maria had developed the tools to manage those triggers in a healthy way.

- **Calm Responses Disempowered Her Ex**: By choosing calm, measured responses (or choosing not to respond at all), Maria disarmed her ex-husband's attempts to provoke her. His usual tactics of criticism and passive-aggressive comments no longer escalated into heated arguments, which diminished his control over their interactions.

- **Emotional Resilience:** Over time, Maria's emotional resilience grew. She felt more confident handling difficult conversations and no longer felt drained after interacting with her ex-husband. This resilience extended beyond her relationship with her ex—it impacted her work, friendships, and parenting, allowing her to approach challenges with a calmer mindset.

- **Reclaiming Her Power:** Most importantly, Maria reclaimed her emotional power. Her ex-husband's criticisms no longer affected her self-worth or decision-making. She felt empowered, knowing she had control over her reactions and that his words no longer dictated her emotional state.

Key Takeaways:

Awareness of Emotional Triggers: Maria's ability to recognize her specific triggers (criticism of her parenting) was crucial in learning how to regulate her responses.

The Power of Pausing: Pausing before responding gave Maria the time to reflect and choose a calm, constructive response, which de-escalated confrontational situations.

Setting Boundaries: By setting clear emotional boundaries and refusing to engage in toxic conversations, Maria protected her emotional well-being and limited her ex-husband's ability to manipulate her.

Emotional Resilience: Maria's emotional resilience grew through consistent mindfulness practice, cognitive restructuring, and reflection. She no longer felt controlled by her emotions or her ex-husband's comments.

Chapter Wrap-up

In this chapter, you've learned that regulating your emotions is not just about controlling your reactions but reclaiming your power. By identifying your emotional triggers, practicing mindfulness, and choosing calm responses, you can disarm manipulative tactics and protect your mental well-being. Emotional resilience is the ultimate form of empowerment, giving you the strength to face challenges with confidence and grace. Key lessons include:

- **Identifying Emotional Triggers:** Understanding what specific situations or comments provoke emotional reactions is the first step to managing those triggers. Awareness gives you the power to prepare and respond intentionally.

- **Using Cognitive Restructuring:** Reframing negative thoughts into more balanced perspectives helps reduce the emotional intensity of difficult situations and stops negative thought cycles before they take hold.

- **Practicing the Pause:** Pausing before reacting creates space for rational decision-making, allowing you to respond calmly instead of impulsively.

- **Setting Emotional Boundaries:** Establishing clear boundaries in conversations and interactions protects your emotional health and limits others' ability to provoke or manipulate you.

- **Mindfulness and Self-Soothing Techniques:** Techniques like deep breathing, mindfulness, and visualization help you manage the physical symptoms of emotional distress, keeping you calm and centered during tense moments.

- **Building Emotional Resilience:** Consistently applying these techniques strengthens your emotional resilience over time, helping you handle future emotional triggers with greater control and confidence.

The key takeaway from this chapter is that learning to regulate your emotional responses can help you reclaim your power in difficult situations, disarm manipulative tactics, and protect your mental well-being.

In the next chapter, we'll explore **Mindset**—how to shift from a reactive victim to an empowered survivor.

Chapter 6

Mindset: Shifting from Victim to Empowered Co-Parent

"You may not control all the events that happen to you, but you can decide not to be reduced by them." – Maya Angelou

Co-parenting with a narcissist can make you feel powerless, constantly at the mercy of their manipulative tactics. It's easy to fall into the role of the victim, feeling trapped in a cycle of emotional turmoil and conflict. But what if the key to reclaiming your peace and emotional freedom lies not in changing the narcissist, but in changing your mindset? In this chapter, you will learn how to shift from feeling like a victim to stepping into your power as an empowered co-parent. This transformation is about changing your thoughts and reclaiming control over your emotions, responses, and overall well-being.

The mindset shift from victim to empowered co-parent is vital to reclaiming your peace and authority in the co-parenting dynamic. This transformation doesn't happen overnight, but it's possible with the right tools, affirmations, and practices. In the following sections, we'll explore practical strategies to reframe your thinking, challenge the negative narrative that keeps you stuck, and cultivate a mindset that allows you to thrive despite the challenges of co-parenting with a narcissist.

Recognizing the Victim Mentality

The first step in shifting your mindset is recognizing the signs of a victim mentality. When you're stuck in this mindset, you might find yourself constantly feeling helpless, blaming the narcissistic ex for all your struggles, and doubting your ability to navigate the co-parenting relationship effectively. This mentality keeps you focused on what's being done to you rather than what you can do for yourself. Here are some common signs:

Blaming others for your emotional state

- Example: "My ex is making my life miserable. If they weren't so manipulative, I'd be happy."

- **Empowered shift:** "I am responsible for how I react, and I can choose to protect my emotional well-being."

Feeling powerless or stuck

- Example: "There's nothing I can do to stop this; I'm completely at their mercy."

- **Empowered shift:** "I can't control their behavior, but I can control how I respond and set boundaries."

Focusing on past wrongs

- Example: "They've always manipulated me, and I've never been able to stand up to them."

- **Empowered shift:** "I've learned from the past, and I'm ready to assert myself now."

Believing you have no options

Example: "I just have to put up with this for the kids' sake; there's no other way."

Empowered shift: "I can create healthier boundaries protecting my children and myself."

Waiting for external change

- Example: "If only they would change, everything would be better."

- **Empowered shift:** "Change begins with me. I can choose to stop engaging in their manipulative tactics."

Challenging these negative beliefs is essential to break free from the victim mentality. Ask yourself: "Am I giving away my power by letting the narcissist control my emotions?" Acknowledging that you have the power to choose how you react is the first step toward reclaiming your personal authority.

Shifting Your Perspective from Helplessness to Empowerment

Once you've recognized the patterns of victim thinking, the next step is actively shifting your perspective. Instead of focusing on what you can't control — the narcissist's behavior, the conflict, or the manipulation — focus on what you can control: your reactions, your boundaries, and your mindset.

One powerful strategy for shifting your perspective is reframing the narrative. Rather than viewing yourself as a victim of circumstances, see yourself as a survivor with the strength and resilience to navigate these challenges. Every time the narcissist attempts to provoke you, instead of falling into old patterns of emotional reactivity, remind yourself: ***"I am in control of my emotions and my responses."***

Affirmations and Daily Practices for Empowerment

Affirmations are a simple yet powerful tool for establishing and reinforcing an empowerment mindset. By repeating positive, empowering statements, you gradually rewire your brain to focus on your strengths rather than your limitations.

Here are a few affirmations to incorporate into your daily routine:

- "I am in control of my emotions and my reactions."
- "I am strong, capable, and resilient."
- "I choose peace over conflict."
- "I am worthy of respect and will not allow anyone to take

my power."

Start each day by saying these affirmations out loud, ideally in front of a mirror. Over time, these positive statements will help you internalize a mindset of empowerment and confidence.

Another helpful practice is journaling. Set aside a few minutes each day to write down any situations where you felt like the victim, and then reframe those experiences from a position of empowerment. For example, instead of writing, "My ex manipulated me again today," try reframing it as, "I recognized my ex's manipulative behavior and chose not to engage." By consistently reframing your experiences, you will shift your narrative from victimhood to empowerment.

Addressing Common Fears and Challenges

As you begin this transformation, it's natural to encounter fears and resistance. Here are some common fears you might face and how to reframe them:

Fear of Losing Control

Thought: "If I don't keep the peace, things will spiral out of control."

Reframe: "True control comes from setting boundaries and protecting my emotional well-being, not avoiding conflict at all costs."

Fear of Escalating Conflict

Thought: "If I stand up for myself, it will make the situation worse."

Reframe: "Standing up for myself calmly and assertively is not about escalating conflict—it's about protecting my peace and self-respect."

Fear of Feeling Guilty for Setting Boundaries

Thought: "I feel guilty when I set boundaries, as if I'm being too harsh."

Reframe: "Setting boundaries is an act of self-care, not selfishness. It's necessary for my well-being and the well-being of my children."

Fear of Disapproval

Thought: "They'll be angry or think I'm unreasonable if I enforce boundaries."

Reframe: "Their reaction is not my responsibility. I am responsible for maintaining my emotional health and keeping the co-parenting relationship respectful."

Fear of Losing Peace

Thought: "It's better to avoid confrontation so I can keep the peace."

Reframe: "Peace built on suppressing my needs is not real peace. True peace comes from respecting myself and standing up for my well-being."

Fear of Being Judged

Thought: "What if others think I'm too difficult or demanding when I set boundaries?"

Reframe: "I cannot control others' opinions, but I can control how I take care of myself. Setting healthy boundaries is a sign of strength, not weakness."

These fears often stem from a deep-seated belief that you must maintain peace at all costs, even at the expense of your emotional well-being. However, standing up for yourself with calm, clear boundaries protects your emotional health and maintains control of your responses.

It's important to remember that standing in your power doesn't mean escalating conflict; it means refusing to let the narcissist control your emotional state. By setting clear boundaries and enforcing them calmly, you maintain control over your life without being drawn into unnecessary drama.

A common challenge in this mindset shift is overcoming the fear of confrontation. Narcissists thrive on conflict, and the idea of asserting yourself can feel intimidating. However, reframing confrontation as simply enforcing your boundaries can make the process feel less daunting. It's not about fighting or getting into arguments; it's about calmly and assertively protecting your peace.

Practical Steps to Empowerment

The following steps can help you reinforce the mindset shift from victim to empowered co-parent:

1. **Identify Your Triggers:** Narcissists know how to push your emotional buttons, so recognizing your triggers is crucial. When you can identify the situations that tend to provoke you, you can prepare yourself to respond with calm and control.

2. **Practice the Pause:** Before responding when confronted with manipulation or conflict. This pause allows you to collect your thoughts, regulate your emotions, and respond from a place of empowerment rather than reactivity.

3. **Set Clear Boundaries:** Boundaries are essential for protecting your emotional well-being. Decide ahead of time what behaviors you will and won't tolerate, and stick to those boundaries confidently. When the narcissist tries to cross them, respond calmly but firmly, reminding them of your boundary without engaging in conflict.

4. **Focus on What You Can Control:** You can't control the narcissist's behavior, but you can control how you react to it. Focus on your responses, boundaries, and the environment you create for your children.

5. **Build a Support Network:** Surround yourself with supportive friends, family, or a therapist who understands your situation. Having a solid support system can make it easier to maintain your empowerment mindset, even when the narcissist tries to wear you down.

The Power of Reclaiming Your Narrative

Reclaiming your narrative is one of the most liberating aspects of this mindset shift. The narcissist may try to define you as powerless, emotional, or incapable, but you get to decide who you are. By reclaiming your narrative, you can redefine yourself as empowered, resilient, and in control of your emotional landscape.

This mindset shift will not only help you navigate your co-parenting relationship with more confidence, but it will also model emotional resilience for your children. When they see you responding to conflict with calm and confidence, they will learn how to manage their own emotions in a healthy way.

Case Study: Allysa's Journey from Victim to Empowered Co-parent

Allysa is a 38-year-old mother of two who has been co-parenting with her narcissistic ex-husband, Eli, for three years. Their relationship was emotionally abusive, with Eli often using manipulation and gaslighting to maintain control over Allysa during their marriage. After their divorce, Allysa continued to struggle with Eli's manipulative tactics, especially during co-parenting decisions. She frequently found herself emotionally drained, reactive, and feeling powerless in their interactions. Eli's behavior, such as making last-minute changes to visitation schedules and criticizing Allysa's parenting in front of the children, left her feeling like a victim of his control even after the separation.

Initial Struggles: For the first year post-divorce, Allysa allowed Eli's behavior to dictate her emotional responses. When he would criticize her, she would become defensive and angry, often leading to explosive arguments. When he made unexpected changes to the children's schedules, she would panic, unable to push back or assert her own needs. Over time, this constant emotional upheaval made Allysa feel stuck, believing she had no choice but to endure the co-parenting conflict for the sake of her children.

Allysa often thought, "I can't do anything about this. Eli will never change." This reinforced her sense of helplessness. She believed the only solution was for Eli to stop being manipulative, but she felt powerless to make that happen.

The Shift Begins: After reaching a breaking point, Allysa sought help from a therapist who specialized in narcissistic abuse and co-parenting issues. In their sessions, Allysa learned the importance of shifting her mindset from victimhood to empowerment. Her therapist introduced her to the idea that while she could not control Eli's behavior, she had complete control over her own responses and emotional well-being.

Together, they identified Allysa's emotional triggers. These included Eli's belittling comments and his last-minute schedule changes for Allysa. Once these triggers were clear, Allysa and her therapist worked on reframing her negative thoughts and practicing emotional regulation techniques.

Allysa's Action Plan:

To begin her journey toward empowerment, Allysa started implementing the following steps:

1. **Reframing Negative Thoughts:** Instead of thinking, "Eli is ruining my life," Allysa began to reframe her thoughts into more empowering ones, such as, "I am in control of how I respond to this situation."

2. **Setting Boundaries:** Allysa realized she had never clearly set boundaries with Eli regarding communication and scheduling. She set firm boundaries around how and when they would communicate about the children. She informed Eli that from now on, all communication would be through email, and she would only respond to non-urgent texts or calls within agreed-upon hours.

3. **Affirmations for Empowerment:** Allysa incorporated daily affirmations into her routine to reinforce her new mindset. Every

morning, she repeated affirmations like, "I am in control of my emotions" and "I deserve peace and respect in my co-parenting relationship."

4. **Gray Rock Method:** Allysa also learned about the Gray Rock Method, a technique designed to minimize emotional reactions when dealing with a manipulative person. When Eli tried to provoke her emotionally, Allysa would respond with brief, neutral comments like, "I understand" or "Noted," without engaging further.

5. **Practicing Emotional Regulation:** Allysa began practicing mindfulness techniques to manage her emotional responses. She learned to pause before reacting and take deep breaths to calm herself before responding to Eli's provocations.

Results and Growth: Within a few months, Allysa noticed significant changes in how she handled interactions with Eli. She could stop arguing emotionally by using the Gray Rock Method and maintaining her boundaries. When Eli criticized her parenting, instead of reacting defensively, Allysa calmly stated, "I'm doing what I believe is best for the kids," and ended the conversation.

Allysa also noticed that her children were less anxious after exchanges with their father. They began to mirror her calm demeanor, and the emotional atmosphere in her household became more peaceful.

One of the most significant breakthroughs for Allysa came when Eli tried to change their holiday plans at the last minute, as he had done many times before. Instead of panicking, Allysa calmly replied that the original schedule would remain in place and did not engage further. Eli pushed back, but Allysa held firm, repeating her boundary without escalating the conflict. Eventually, Eli backed down, and for the first time, Allysa felt empowered in her co-parenting relationship.

Through consistent practice of reframing her thoughts, setting boundaries, and using emotional regulation techniques, Allysa shifted from feeling like a victim of her ex-husband's manipulation to feeling empowered in their co-parenting relationship. She no longer allowed Eli's behavior to dictate her emotional state. By focusing on what she could control—her reactions and boundaries—Allysa regained her peace of mind and set a strong example of resilience for her children.

Chapter Wrap-up

In this chapter, we explored the critical shift from a victim mentality to an empowered mindset in co-parenting with a narcissist. The key to this transformation is recognizing that while you cannot control your ex-partner's behavior, you have complete control over your emotional responses and boundaries.

We began by identifying the signs of a victim mentality, including feelings of helplessness, emotional reactivity, and the belief that the narcissist holds all the power. From there, we discussed how recognizing and managing emotional triggers is the first step to regaining control.

The chapter then introduced practical techniques for reframing negative thoughts, including using positive affirmations, setting and enforcing clear boundaries, and practicing emotional regulation through methods like the Gray Rock Method. These strategies allow you to regain control of your emotional well-being and model empowered behavior for your children.

Finally, we emphasized the importance of self-compassion and recognizing setbacks as part of the empowerment journey. Empowerment is a process that requires consistency and patience, but with each step, you become more resilient and better equipped to handle co-parenting challenges with strength and confidence.

By applying these practices, you'll begin to see a profound shift in how you navigate your relationship with your narcissistic ex-partner, moving from a place of victimhood to empowerment.

In the next chapter, you will learn how to build lasting emotional resilience through the **Practice** of new daily habits. This will ensure that the empowerment you gain through mindset shifts will carry you forward in the long term, providing peace for both you and your children.

Chapter 7

Practices: Building Daily Habits for Strength

"You gain strength, courage, and confidence by every experience in which you really stop to look fear in the face. You are able to say to yourself, 'I lived through this horror. I can take the next thing that comes along.'" —
Eleanor Roosevelt

In the whirlwind of co-parenting, especially with a narcissistic ex-partner, the idea of establishing new habits might feel overwhelming. But what if the key to emotional strength isn't in making huge changes but in the simple, daily actions that ground you? Mindfulness, journaling, and self-care may seem insignificant when weighed against the stress of your circumstances, but these practices, done consistently, form the bedrock of your emotional fortitude. The habits you develop today will be the cornerstone of the peace and resilience you seek for both you and your children.

As we explore the daily practices that foster emotional strength, you'll discover how even small moments of mindfulness, the act of putting pen to paper and carving out time for self-care can shift the tide in your favor. Let's explore these powerful habits and how they can fit seamlessly into your busy life.

Building Emotional Fortitude Through Mindfulness

Mindfulness is the art of staying present in the moment, fully aware of your thoughts, feelings, and surroundings without judgment. When co-parenting with a narcissist, staying emotionally detached and focused on the present can be challenging. Narcissists often provoke reactions by triggering old wounds or manipulating your emotions. However, mindfulness provides a tool to navigate these provocations without getting emotionally entangled.

Practicing mindfulness doesn't require hours of meditation or sitting cross-legged in silence. In fact, it can be as simple as spending five minutes a day focusing on your breath, observing your thoughts, or grounding yourself in the present moment. In doing this, you train your mind to remain calm and focused even when external circumstances become chaotic. The steps below will guide you through incorporating mindfulness into your daily routine.

Morning grounding exercise: Before you jump into the day's tasks, spend five minutes practicing deep breathing or a body scan. This will center your mind and set the tone for a calm, focused day.

Practice Deep Breathing:

    1. Sit or lie down in a comfortable position.

2. Inhale deeply through your nose for a count of four, filling your lungs and expanding your belly.

3. Hold your breath for a count of four.

4. Slowly exhale through your mouth for a count of four, letting all the air out.

5. Repeat this cycle for a few minutes, focusing on the sensation of your breath.

This practice helps you focus on the present moment, reduces anxiety, and improves concentration.

Practice a Body Scan:

1. Lie down or sit comfortably with your eyes closed.

2. Start by focusing on your toes. Notice any sensations (warmth, tingling, or tension) without trying to change them.

3. Slowly move your attention up through your body, from your feet, legs, hips, back, shoulders, arms, neck, and face.

4. As you move through each area, consciously relax that part of your body if you notice tension.

5. Continue this process until you've scanned your entire body, paying attention to how each part feels.

The body scan is excellent for reducing physical stress, calming the mind, and improving your connection with your body.

Mindful parenting moments: When you're with your children, take a few seconds to notice your surroundings. Listen to their laughter, feel the texture of their hands, and stay present in that connection. This helps anchor you in positive moments.

Evening reflection: At the end of each day, take a few minutes to reflect on the emotions you felt, without judgment. Observe how you reacted to certain situations and identify moments where mindfulness could have helped you stay grounded.

When done consistently, these small practices build your capacity to respond to challenges calmly rather than react impulsively. Over time, mindfulness becomes your first line of defense against emotional manipulation.

The Power of Journaling for Clarity and Emotional Release

Journaling offers a safe space to process your emotions and reflect on your daily experiences. It provides a way to release pent-up emotions and clarify the patterns that trigger your stress. Co-parenting with a narcissist often involves navigating complex emotions—anger, guilt, frustration, and sadness. These emotions can build up without a healthy outlet, leading to emotional exhaustion.

Writing your thoughts down on paper can help you organize your feelings and understand them better. It's not just about venting but about gaining insights into your emotional responses. For example, after a difficult interaction with your ex, you might journal about what was said, how it made you feel, and how you responded. Over time, you'll start noticing patterns in both their behavior and your reactions, helping you break the emotional reactivity cycle.

Practical journaling tips for busy parents:

- **Daily reflection:** Set aside 10 minutes at the end of each day to write about your feelings, frustrations, and victories. This small habit can provide immense emotional relief.

- **Gratitude journaling:** Along with reflecting on the challenges, write down at least three things you're grateful for each day. This shifts your focus from stress to positive experiences, fostering a mindset of resilience.

- **Trigger identification:** After a difficult interaction, jot down what triggered your emotions. By recognizing these triggers, you can prepare for similar situations in the future and respond with more control.

Journaling doesn't need to be a long, drawn-out process. Even writing a few sentences each day can help clear your mind and build emotional awareness.

Self-Care: Nurturing Yourself to Build Resilience

Self-care is often the first thing to go when life gets overwhelming. As a parent navigating the complexities of co-parenting with a narcissist, it may feel selfish or impossible to prioritize your own needs. However, self-care is not a luxury—it's a necessity. Caring for yourself builds the emotional and physical stamina needed to face daily challenges with strength and clarity.

Self-care doesn't mean you need to book a weekend spa retreat (though if you can, go for it!). It's about finding small, consistent ways to nourish your body and mind amidst the chaos of daily life. Whether it's taking a 15-minute walk, enjoying a quiet cup of tea, or reading a chapter of a book, these moments recharge you, allowing you to show up as your best self for both your children and yourself.

How to incorporate self-care into a busy schedule:

- **Micro-breaks:** Throughout the day, take short 5-minute breaks to step outside, stretch, or simply close your eyes and breathe deeply. These micro-breaks help reset your mind and reduce stress.

- **Create a bedtime routine:** Wind down with a simple routine that helps you relax before bed—whether it's reading, journaling, or listening to calming music. This can improve your sleep quality, which is crucial for emotional resilience.

- **Exercise regularly:** You don't need to commit to an hour at the gym. Even a 10-minute walk or stretching session can make a big difference in your mental and physical health. Regular movement boosts your mood and helps manage stress.

By prioritizing self-care, you set a powerful example for your children. You show them that taking time for yourself is okay, and you'll have the energy and emotional stability needed to be fully present for them.

The Long-Term Benefits of Consistent Practice

The daily habits of mindfulness, journaling, and self-care may seem small on their own, but over time, they become a powerful force for emotional stability and strength. These practices not only help you manage the challenges of co-parenting with a narcissist but also equip you with the tools to maintain peace in the long run.

Consistency is key. The more you integrate these habits into your daily routine, the more natural they will become, even during the most stressful times. They will serve as a buffer against emotional exhaustion, giving you the clarity and strength to make decisions that benefit both you and your children.

In the long term, these habits create a foundation for resilience. You'll find you're less reactive to your ex-partner's manipulations and better equipped to handle co-parenting challenges gracefully and confidently. As your emotional strength grows, so will your ability to provide your children a stable, nurturing environment.

Case Study: Chelsea's Journey to Emotional Resilience Through Daily Habits

Chelsea, a 33-year-old mother of two, had been co-parenting with her narcissistic ex-husband for three years. The ongoing conflict, manipulation, and power struggles left her feeling emotionally drained, constantly reacting to her ex's provocations. She was overwhelmed, anxious, and feared the impact her stress was having on her children.

Chelsea knew she needed to change how she handled the emotional challenges, but she didn't know where to start. After reading about mindfulness, journaling, and self-care in a book on co-parenting, she decided to implement these practices, hoping they could provide relief.

The Challenge: Chelsea's biggest obstacle was time. She was already balancing full-time work and caring for her children, leaving little room for self-care. Additionally, she struggled with feelings of guilt—she felt selfish for taking time for herself when so much of her attention needed to be on her children. But she also realized that living in constant stress wasn't healthy for her or her kids.

Implementation:

1. **Mindfulness:** Chelsea started with small, daily mindfulness exercises. She set aside five minutes each morning to practice deep breathing before her children woke up. Instead of diving straight into her to-do list, she focused on her breath and quieted her mind. Throughout the day, she tried to remain aware of her emotions, especially during stressful interactions with her ex.

2. **Journaling:** In the evenings, Chelsea spent 10 minutes writing in a journal after the kids were in bed. She used this time to reflect on her day, especially moments when she felt triggered by her ex's behavior. Writing about these incidents helped her understand her emotional reactions and identify patterns in her interactions. Over time, journaling became an emotional release, providing clarity and helping her process difficult feelings.

3. **Self-Care:** Chelsea realized that self-care didn't have to involve long, luxurious activities. She started with small things—drinking tea in the evening, taking short walks during her lunch break, and spending a few minutes reading before bed. These small acts made

her feel more grounded and gave her something to look forward to each day.

Results:

- **Improved Emotional Control:** Within a few weeks, Chelsea noticed that her emotional reactivity had decreased. When her ex-partner tried to provoke her, she remained calm, responding with a level head rather than reacting impulsively. Her mindfulness practice helped her pause before responding, giving her time to choose a calm, measured reaction.

- **Clarity and Emotional Release Through Journaling:** Journaling allowed Chelsea to see patterns in her ex's behavior and her reactions. She realized that many of his provocations followed a predictable pattern. Once she understood this, it became easier to detach emotionally. Writing down her thoughts also helped her release pent-up frustrations, which led to less stress and anxiety.

- **Resilience and Self-Care:** The small acts of self-care Chelsea incorporated into her day made a big difference. She felt more balanced and energized, which helped her handle the challenges of co-parenting. Taking time for herself didn't feel selfish anymore; instead, it became a way to recharge, making her more present and patient with her children.

- **Positive Impact on Her Children:** As Chelsea's emotional resilience grew, her children began to notice the change. They saw her handling conflicts with their father calmly, which reduced their anxiety. The household became more peaceful, and Chelsea felt more confident creating a nurturing space for her kids.

Through small, consistent habits—mindfulness, journaling, and self-care—Chelsea was able to reclaim her emotional strength. These daily practices didn't eliminate the challenges of co-parenting with a narcissist, but they gave her the tools to navigate those challenges with grace and resilience. Chelsea's journey demonstrates that building emotional fortitude is possible even with limited time, and the benefits extend beyond personal well-being to positively affect the entire family.

Chapter Wrap-up

In this chapter, we explored how small, consistent habits—mindfulness, journaling, and self-care—can build emotional strength and resilience, especially for those navigating the challenges of co-parenting with a narcissist.

- **Mindfulness:** Practicing mindfulness, even for just 5 minutes a day, helps reduce emotional reactivity and fosters calmness. Simple mindfulness exercises, like focusing on your breath or being fully present during routine activities, can lead to greater emotional control.

- **Journaling:** Journaling offers a powerful way to process emotions and gain clarity. Writing down thoughts and reflecting on emotional triggers can help you recognize patterns, reduce stress, and improve your responses to difficult situations.

- **Self-Care:** Prioritizing self-care doesn't require extensive time or effort. Small, daily acts of self-care—like taking short walks or enjoying quiet moments—are crucial for maintaining emotional balance and preventing burnout.

Through these practices, you'll develop long-term emotional fortitude. The benefits of these habits extend beyond yourself, creating a more peaceful and stable environment for your children. Committing to these routines builds the foundation for lasting emotional resilience, even in the face of co-parenting challenges.

Next, we'll dive into the **Obstacles** you may encounter as you strive to maintain these habits and how to overcome them with confidence and resilience.

Chapter 8

Obstacles: Navigating Legal, Financial, and Emotional Hurdles

"The greater the obstacle, the more glory in overcoming it." – Molière

In this chapter, we'll explore the common legal, financial, and emotional hurdles you are likely to face while co-parenting with a narcissist. From manipulative legal tactics to financial games and the emotional chaos that comes with it, these obstacles can feel overwhelming. But there is hope. With the right strategies, preparation, and support system, you can navigate these challenges confidently, all while focusing on your children's well-being.

By the end of this chapter, you will have the tools to tackle each hurdle head-on, reclaiming control over your life and parenting journey.

Legal Manipulations: When the Court Becomes Their Playground

One of the most frustrating aspects of co-parenting with a narcissist is the way they use the legal system to maintain control. Narcissists thrive on conflict, and the courtroom provides them with an ideal battleground. They will drag you into court over the smallest of issues, twist facts, and weaponize legal documents to keep you emotionally drained and financially exhausted.

Common Legal Tactics Narcissists Use:

1. **Endless Custody Disputes:** Narcissists often refuse to settle on custody agreements, filing motions or petitions that disrupt the stability of your parenting schedule.

2. **False Allegations:** They may accuse you of neglect or abuse, manipulating the legal system to paint you as an unfit parent.

3. **Withholding Financial Support:** Refusing to pay child support, manipulating joint finances, or hiding assets is another way they keep control and create financial stress.

4. **Violation of Court Orders:** Narcissists frequently ignore legal agreements, knowing it will force you back into costly legal battles.

Strategies to Overcome Legal Challenges:

- **Document Everything:** Keep a detailed log of interactions with your ex, including emails, texts, and any violations of court orders. This documentation can be critical in court.

- **Work with a Knowledgeable Lawyer:** A lawyer understanding narcissistic behavior is essential. They will know how to counter the manipulative tactics and prevent you from getting dragged into unnecessary legal battles.

- **Stay Emotionally Detached in Court:** Narcissists feed off emotional reactions. Keep calm and composed during hearings to avoid giving them the satisfaction of seeing you rattled.

- **Use the Law to Your Advantage:** Familiarize yourself with legal protections and resources to help you maintain boundaries and ensure the court holds your ex accountable for any violations.

By anticipating these legal tactics and taking proactive steps, you can prevent the narcissist from using the court system as a tool for control.

Financial Control: Breaking Free from Economic Manipulation

Financial control is another weapon narcissists frequently use to maintain power in a co-parenting relationship. They may withhold child support, drain joint accounts, or leave you with debts. These financial tactics are designed to make you feel powerless, but there are ways to regain control.

Common Financial Challenges:

- **Refusal to Pay Child Support:** Narcissists often try to avoid their financial obligations, either by delaying payments or disputing the amount.

- **Using Financial Dependency as Leverage:** They may create financial dependency by cutting off access to joint accounts or refusing to contribute to shared expenses.

- **Sudden Financial Demands:** Narcissists can create financial crises, such as refusing to pay for medical expenses or schooling, knowing it will create stress and instability.

Strategies for Overcoming Financial Manipulation:

1. **Separate Finances as Soon as Possible:** If you haven't done so already, ensure all joint accounts are closed, and set up your own bank account. This minimizes their ability to control your financial situation.

2. **Enforce Child Support Agreements:** If your ex refuses to pay child support, take legal action. Mechanisms exist to enforce these payments, including garnishing wages.

3. **Create a Financial Safety Net:** Build an emergency fund, even if you can only contribute a small amount at a time. This will provide financial security when your ex tries to create financial chaos.

4. **Track Every Expense:** Keep a detailed record of all child-related expenses, including receipts. If you need to go back to court, this evidence will support your claims for additional financial contributions from your ex.

While financial manipulation can feel overwhelming, these strategies will give you the confidence to regain control of your finances and reduce your ex's influence in this area.

Emotional Manipulation: Maintaining Your Sanity

The emotional toll of co-parenting with a narcissist is perhaps the most exhausting challenge of all. Narcissists thrive on creating emotional chaos, using manipulation, guilt, and gaslighting to undermine your confidence as a parent and as an individual.

Common Emotional Hurdles:

- **Constant Conflict:** Narcissists are relentless in creating drama. They may send angry texts, provoke arguments, or undermine your parenting decisions in front of your children.

- **Gaslighting:** This is a form of manipulation where they make you question your own reality. They might deny previous agreements, shift blame onto you, or distort facts to make you feel you're the problem.

- **Emotional Manipulation Through the Children:** Narcissists often use children as pawns, turning them against you or manipulating their emotions to make you feel guilty or inadequate.

Strategies for Managing Emotional Challenges:

- **Practice Emotional Detachment:** This doesn't mean you stop caring about the situation, but rather that you stop engaging emotionally with the narcissist. The "gray rock method," where you respond with short, non-emotional answers, can prevent them from gaining satisfaction from your reactions.

- **Set Clear Boundaries:** Decide what you will and will not engage with in advance. For example, if your ex starts to argue or send inflammatory messages, refuse to engage. You are not obligated to respond to every provocation.

- **Focus on Your Children:** Narcissists want to pull your focus away from your children and onto the conflict. Refocus your energy on creating a stable, nurturing environment for your kids, even if your ex is trying to create chaos.

- **Lean on a Support System:** Whether it's a therapist, a close friend, or a support group for those dealing with narcissistic abuse, having people who understand what you're going through can provide emotional strength and perspective.

The Importance of a Support System: You Don't Have to Do This Alone

One of the most crucial tools in your arsenal when co-parenting with a narcissist is a strong support system. This could include friends, family, professionals, or support groups. The emotional and psychological toll of dealing with a narcissist can feel isolating, but it's important to remember that you are not alone.

How to Build and Maintain a Support System:

1. **Professional Support:** A therapist who specializes in narcissistic abuse can help you manage the emotional challenges and provide strategies for maintaining your mental health.

2. **Legal Support:** Having a lawyer who understands narcissistic behavior can ensure that your legal rights are protected and help

you navigate the complexities of custody and financial battles.

3. **Community Support:** Consider joining a support group of other parents going through similar experiences. These groups can provide emotional validation, practical advice, and a sense of camaraderie.

4. **Friends and Family:** While your immediate circle may not fully understand what you're dealing with, sharing your struggles with trusted friends or family can provide emotional relief and perspective.

Case Study: Navigating Legal, Financial, and Emotional Hurdles with a Narcissistic Ex

Emma, a 33-year-old mother of two, struggled with co-parenting her children after divorcing her narcissistic ex-husband, James. Following the divorce, James began to use legal, financial, and emotional tactics to maintain control over Emma and the children. Emma felt overwhelmed, constantly entangled in unnecessary legal battles, financially stretched due to unpaid child support, and emotionally drained by James's manipulative behavior.

Legal Hurdles: Constant Court Battles

James frequently violated the custody agreement, showing up late to pick up the children or refusing to return them on time. He filed multiple false claims, accusing Emma of neglect and pushing her into court at every opportunity. These constant legal battles left Emma anxious and drained, unsure how to manage the escalating conflict.

Solution: Emma decided to start documenting every interaction with James, including missed pick-up times, violations of the custody agreement, and false allegations. She kept a detailed log of text messages, emails, and phone calls, along with any supporting evidence. Emma also hired a lawyer who specialized in high-conflict custody battles. This lawyer understood narcissistic behavior and helped Emma present her well-documented evidence in court.

Outcome: The court ruled in Emma's favor, dismissing James's false claims. More importantly, Emma's consistent documentation and calm demeanor during court appearances significantly reduced the frequency of future legal disputes.

Key Takeaway: By documenting every legal violation and working with an experienced lawyer, Emma regained control over the legal battles, reducing her ex's ability to manipulate her through the court system.

Financial Hurdles: Withholding Child Support

James also attempted to control Emma financially by withholding child support. He frequently claimed he couldn't afford to make payments or sent reduced amounts, knowing this would create a financial strain for Emma and their children, leaving Emma struggling to cover basic expenses like school fees and medical bills.

Solution: Emma consulted her lawyer about enforcing the child support agreement. After several attempts to negotiate directly with James, Emma filed a motion with the court to garnish his wages, ensuring child support payments were made automatically. She also worked with a financial advisor to create a strict budget, setting up a separate bank account for her children's expenses to safeguard her finances.

Outcome: The court ruled in Emma's favor, enforcing wage garnishment to secure consistent child support payments. With her finances under control and her ex no longer able to manipulate her through money, Emma felt more secure and able to focus on her children's well-being.

Key Takeaway: By legally enforcing child support and separating finances, Emma regained her financial independence and reduced her ex's control over her through money.

Emotional Hurdles: Manipulation and Gaslighting

Throughout their co-parenting journey, James frequently tried to manipulate Emma emotionally. He sent texts accusing her of being a bad mother, used guilt to manipulate her into changing the custody schedule, and often involved the children in their conflicts by badmouthing her in front of them. Emma felt emotionally exhausted and found herself constantly reacting to James's provocations.

Solution: Emma began working with a therapist who specialized in narcissistic abuse. She learned to practice the Gray Rock Method, responding to James's manipulative texts with brief, unemotional answers and only engaging in communication that involved the children's immediate needs. She also set firm boundaries, choosing not to respond to non-urgent messages outside of specific hours and refusing to be drawn into unnecessary conflicts.

Outcome: Over time, Emma's emotional detachment took away James's power to manipulate her. As she stopped reacting emotionally, James's attempts to create conflict decreased. Emma also focused on providing a stable, nurturing environment for her children, ensuring they felt safe and loved, even amid co-parenting challenges.

Key Takeaway: Practicing emotional detachment and setting clear communication boundaries helped Emma protect her mental health and reduce the emotional manipulation from her narcissistic ex.

Building a Support System

Initially, Emma felt isolated and overwhelmed, believing she had to face these challenges alone. However, she realized that building a support system was crucial for navigating co-parenting with a narcissist. She reached out to trusted friends and family members, joined a local support group for parents in high-conflict co-parenting situations, and continued her therapy sessions.

Solution: Emma's support group offered her a sense of community and understanding. Hearing other parents' stories gave her practical advice on managing difficult situations. Her therapist helped her build emotional resilience, while her friends and family provided much-needed emotional support, helping her navigate the most challenging moments.

Outcome: With a strong support system, Emma no longer felt isolated. She felt more empowered to handle the legal, financial, and emotional hurdles James threw her way. Having a network of trusted people made her stronger, more resilient, and better able to protect herself and her children.

Key Takeaway: Building a solid support system gave Emma the strength and resources she needed to handle the challenges of co-parenting with a narcissist and provided a safety net during difficult times.

Emma's journey through the legal, financial, and emotional challenges of co-parenting with a narcissistic ex was tough. Still, she regained control over her life by applying strategies such as documentation, financial independence, emotional detachment, and building a strong support system. Emma's experience demonstrates that while co-parenting with a narcissist is never easy, it is possible to create a more stable and peaceful environment for yourself and your children by taking proactive steps to protect your well-being.

Chapter Wrap-up

In this chapter, we examined the three primary challenges of co-parenting with a narcissist: legal, financial, and emotional hurdles. Narcissists often use these areas to maintain control and create conflict, but with the right strategies, you can overcome these obstacles and protect your well-being and your children's.

- **Legal Challenges:** Narcissists use the legal system to file false allegations, drag out custody battles, and ignore court orders. The solution lies in documenting every interaction, working with a lawyer who understands narcissistic behavior, and maintaining emotional detachment during legal proceedings.

- **Financial Challenges:** Narcissists manipulate finances by withholding child support or creating crises to destabilize you. You can regain financial control by separating finances, enforcing child support through legal channels, and building a financial safety net for your family.

- **Emotional Challenges:** Narcissists thrive on emotional manipulation, using tactics like gaslighting and turning the children against you. Practicing emotional detachment, setting boundaries, and focusing on your children's well-being will help you stay grounded and resist emotional manipulation.

By using the strategies outlined in this chapter—legal documentation, financial independence, emotional detachment, and building a support system—you can confidently navigate the challenges of co-parenting with a narcissist and maintain control over your life and your children's well-being.

In the next chapter, we will explore **Withdrawal**—how to detach without disengaging from your parental responsibilities. You'll employ techniques like the Gray Rock Method and other ways to protect your emotional well-being while still being a present, supportive parent for your children.

Chapter 9

Withdrawal: Detaching Without Disengaging

"Sometimes letting things go is an act of far greater power than defending or hanging on." – Eckhart Tolle

In the turbulent world of co-parenting with a narcissist, learning to step back emotionally while remaining fully engaged as a parent is a crucial skill. It's not about giving up on your responsibilities or disengaging from your children's lives. Rather, it's about creating a safe emotional space where you can shield yourself from conflict without allowing the narcissist to draw you into their web of manipulation. In this chapter, you will learn how to master emotional detachment while maintaining your essential role as a parent. This skill will protect you and empower you to stay present for your children in the healthiest way possible.

Understanding Emotional Detachment

Emotional detachment often carries a negative connotation. It may evoke images of coldness, indifference, or even neglect. But when dealing with a narcissistic co-parent, detachment becomes a tool of survival. Narcissists thrive on emotional chaos and conflict, and they often use these tactics to maintain control over you. By refusing to engage emotionally, you deny them the fuel they need to manipulate and provoke you. The key is to remain calm and composed despite their provocations.

Detaching doesn't mean you stop caring about your children's well-being or the outcome of co-parenting. Instead, it means removing yourself from the emotional hooks the narcissist uses to control the situation. This chapter will walk you through practical strategies, including the gray rock method, to help you achieve this balance.

The Gray Rock Method: A Simple Yet Powerful Tool

Here's how to practice the Gray Rock Method effectively:

1. **Neutral Responses**: Respond with short, neutral statements when your co-parent attempts to bait you into an argument. For example, a simple "I see" or "That's your opinion" is sufficient if they criticize your parenting. Avoid defending yourself, explaining your actions, or showing any emotional reaction.

2. **Limited Interaction:** Keep your communication to the bare minimum. If you must interact with them, stick to necessary topics like child-related logistics. Avoid any personal discussions or responding to inflammatory comments. The less you engage, the better.

3. **Non-Reactivity:** The Gray Rock Method requires you to re-

main emotionally unresponsive, even when provoked. This can be incredibly difficult, especially when the narcissist knows how to push your buttons. However, with practice, you can train yourself to remain calm and detached in these situations.

By employing the Gray Rock Method, you're not abandoning your responsibilities—you're simply choosing not to feed into the drama. Your focus remains on your children and your emotional health.

Balancing Detachment with Parenting Responsibilities

A common concern for parents learning to detach emotionally is the fear that they may come across as distant or neglectful to their children, which is a misconception. In fact, emotional detachment from the narcissistic co-parent can improve your ability to parent effectively. When not constantly embroiled in conflict, you have more emotional energy to focus on your children.

Here's how you can detach without disengaging from your parenting responsibilities:

1. **Stay Present with Your Children:** Just because you're detaching from your ex doesn't mean detaching from your kids. It's quite the opposite. By stepping back from conflict, you can be more present for your children. You'll have more patience, emotional clarity, and energy to give them the support they need.

2. **Model Healthy Boundaries:** By practicing detachment, you teach your children an invaluable lesson about boundaries. They will witness how you protect your emotional well-being without neglecting your parental duties, thus teaching them that it's

possible to maintain self-respect while fulfilling responsibilities to others.

3. **Create a Calm Environment:** Children are sensitive to the emotional tone of their environment. If they see you constantly stressed, angry, or upset due to interactions with your narcissistic ex, it will affect them. Emotional detachment allows you to create a calm, stable environment for your children, which is essential for their emotional well-being.

Strategies for Maintaining Healthy Communication Boundaries

Communication with a narcissistic co-parent can feel like navigating a minefield. Every conversation seems designed to provoke, frustrate, or manipulate. Establishing and enforcing clear boundaries is essential in these interactions. By detaching emotionally, you can communicate purposefully and clearly without getting dragged into unnecessary conflict.

Here are some strategies for maintaining healthy communication boundaries:

- **Set Clear Limits on Communication:** Define when and how communication will occur. Use written communication such as emails or co-parenting apps, providing a record of the conversation and reducing the likelihood of miscommunication or manipulation.

- **Use "BIFF" Responses:** Keep your responses short and to the point, while maintaining a neutral tone. Avoid any unnecessary detail or emotion in your replies.

- **Do Not Engage with Provocations:** Narcissists often provoke intentionally to pull you into an argument. When you notice this happening, remind yourself that engaging will only escalate the situation. Stick to the facts and end the conversation as quickly as possible.

By following these strategies, you can maintain necessary communication without allowing it to become emotionally draining. You're setting boundaries for yourself and your children, ensuring their emotional space is protected.

The Power of Emotional Detachment

Emotional detachment is not a weakness—it is one of your greatest strengths in navigating the challenges of co-parenting with a narcissist. Detaching emotionally allows you to see situations more clearly, make better decisions for your children, and preserve your mental health. It creates a space where you are no longer at the mercy of your ex's manipulative tactics.

When you master the art of detachment, you gain control over your emotions and reactions. You can choose how to respond, rather than reacting impulsively. This not only disempowers the narcissist but also empowers you to remain grounded and focused on what truly matters—your children.

Detaching without disengaging involves:

- **Prioritizing your mental and emotional health:** Remember, you can't pour from an empty cup. Protecting your emotional well-being makes you a better parent and role model for your children.

- **Staying present for your children:** Detachment doesn't mean you stop caring—it means you stop caring about the wrong things. Your children need you to be emotionally available and steady, not embroiled in conflict with your ex.

- **Maintain strong communication boundaries:** Set the terms for how and when communication occurs and stick to them. Refrain from engaging in provocations to protect your emotional energy and time.

Case Study: The Power of Detachment in Co-Parenting

Jessica, a 38-year-old mother of three, had been co-parenting with her narcissistic ex-husband, David, for two years following their divorce. Every conversation between them quickly escalated into an argument, with David constantly criticizing her parenting and attempting to manipulate her emotionally. Jessica often found herself feeling drained, anxious, and defensive after their interactions, which took a toll on her emotional well-being and left her feeling powerless.

The Challenge: Jessica wanted to create a stable, peaceful environment for her children, but David's relentless attempts to provoke her into conflict made it difficult. He would frequently send aggressive texts, make accusations during drop-offs, and try to undermine her parenting decisions in front of the kids. Jessica felt she had to constantly defend herself, leading to more conflict and stress.

Implementing Detachment:

After reading about emotional detachment and the Gray Rock Method, Jessica decided to try a new approach. She realized that her reactions were fueling David's behavior, and by engaging emotionally, she was giving him the control he sought. Jessica decided to stop reacting to his provocations and instead apply the strategies she had learned.

- **Using the Gray Rock Method:** In her interactions with David, Jessica responded with short, neutral answers. When he criticized her parenting or made hurtful remarks, she would say, "I see," or "Thank you for sharing your thoughts," and then move on. She refused to argue, no matter how personal the attacks became.

- **Setting Boundaries in Communication:** Jessica also set clear communication boundaries. She limited all non-essential communication to a co-parenting app, only discussing child-related matters. If David tried to bring up unrelated topics or provoke her through the app, Jessica would ignore the messages and only respond to relevant ones. When face-to-face, she kept her responses brief and factual, refusing to get drawn into his provocations.

- **Prioritizing Self-Care:** To help herself stay emotionally detached, Jessica built a self-care routine into her daily life. She started practicing mindfulness and meditation to manage her stress and refocus her energy on herself and her children. She also began journaling about her interactions with David, reflecting on what worked and where she could improve her detachment strategy.

The Results: Within a few weeks, Jessica noticed significant changes. David's attempts to provoke her gradually diminished as he realized he was no longer getting the emotional reactions he sought. By remaining calm and neutral, Jessica took away his power to control the situation through manipulation and conflict. Their interactions became more focused on the children, and there was less tension during drop-offs and exchanges.

Jessica also noticed a positive shift in her emotional well-being. She no longer felt anxious before interacting with David, and the reduction in conflict gave her more emotional energy to invest in her children. Her children, in turn, began to thrive in the more peaceful environment, sensing the change in their mother's demeanor and the decrease in parental tension.

Key Takeaways:

1. **Detachment as a Source of Control:** Jessica regained control over her emotions and the co-parenting dynamic by emotionally detaching from David's provocations. The Gray Rock Method allowed her to interact with David without being drawn into conflict, protecting her mental health and setting the tone for more civil communication.

2. **Boundaries as a Protective Measure:** Setting strict communication boundaries helped Jessica avoid unnecessary conflict and stay focused on her parenting responsibilities. By refusing to engage in emotionally charged conversations, she preserved her energy and reduced the opportunities for David to manipulate her.

3. **Self-Care to Support Detachment:** Practicing self-care was crucial for Jessica in maintaining her emotional resilience. Mindfulness, journaling, and focusing on her well-being helped her stay grounded and emotionally strong, even in the face of David's

provocations.

4. **Improved Environment for Children:** Jessica's decision to detach from the conflict with her ex also positively impacted her children. They no longer had to witness their parents arguing or experience the stress of constant tension, creating a healthier, more stable home environment.

Conclusion

Jessica's case demonstrates how mastering emotional detachment, setting firm boundaries, and practicing self-care can transform a high-conflict co-parenting relationship. By taking control of her emotional reactions and refusing to engage in David's manipulative behavior, she created a more peaceful environment for herself and her children. The Gray Rock Method and emotional detachment allowed her to focus on her role as a mother, while significantly reducing the emotional toll of interacting with her narcissistic ex.

Chapter Wrap-up

In this chapter, we explored the concept of emotional detachment as a critical tool for co-parenting with a narcissist. Detaching emotionally doesn't mean abandoning your parenting responsibilities; rather, it allows you to protect your emotional well-being while maintaining your role as a parent. The chapter debunked common myths about emotional detachment, clarifying that it is not a sign of neglect or weakness, but rather a source of strength and protection for yourself and your children. Emotional detachment helps create a more peaceful environment for you and your family, reducing stress and improving overall well-being.

In summary, mastering emotional detachment allows you to withdraw from conflict without disengaging from your parental duties, providing you and your children with a healthier, more peaceful co-parenting dynamic.

Now that you've learned the art of emotional detachment and how to withdraw from conflict without disengaging from your responsibilities as a parent, the next step is to **Enforce** those boundaries with confidence. In the upcoming chapter, we'll dive into the practical strategies you can use to maintain your boundaries, even in the face of persistent manipulation or attempts to violate them.

Chapter 10

Enforcement: Maintaining Boundaries with Confidence

" 'No.' is a complete sentence." — Anne Lamott

In a high-conflict co-parenting dynamic, especially with a narcissistic ex-partner, boundaries are not just helpful—they are essential. Without firm and consistent boundaries, you risk being manipulated, emotionally drained, and losing control over your life and your parenting. This chapter dives into the heart of confidently maintaining boundaries, teaching you how to communicate assertively, document boundary violations, and consistently enforce these limits to protect yourself and your children from further emotional harm.

Establishing boundaries is not a one-time event; it is a continuous practice of holding firm, even when challenged. Without boundaries, your ex will sense your vulnerability and take every opportunity to re-establish control, especially when you begin to detach emotionally. By the end of this chapter, you will understand how to set clear boundaries and consistently enforce them with confidence and grace, ensuring long-term emotional freedom and safety.

Assertive Communication Techniques for Co-Parenting Boundaries

The foundation of boundary enforcement lies in assertive communication. Assertiveness is not about aggression or confrontation—it's about calmly and clearly stating your needs, expectations, and limits without apology. For many, this can be a difficult balance to strike, especially if you've been conditioned to avoid conflict or feel guilt for asserting yourself. However, in co-parenting with a narcissist, assertiveness is key to preventing manipulation and maintaining control over your emotions and decisions.

Here are the main assertive communication techniques that will help you enforce your boundaries effectively:

- **Use "I" Statements:** When you communicate boundaries, focus on how the situation affects you, rather than attacking or blaming your ex-partner. For example, instead of saying, "You're always late, and it's frustrating," try, "I feel disrespected when the schedule is not followed. I need consistency for the sake of the children." This reduces the likelihood of escalation and focuses on the issue at hand, not the person.

- **Stay Emotionally Neutral:** Narcissists thrive on emotional reactions—they see them as opportunities to regain control or draw you into conflict. Maintaining emotional neutrality when enforcing boundaries is essential. Use a calm, even tone of voice, and avoid rising to provocations. Techniques like the Gray Rock Method, where you provide minimal emotional response, can be invaluable in these situations. Remember, emotional detachment doesn't mean you stop caring—it means you protect your peace.

- **Be Clear and Direct:** Vagueness leaves room for manipulation. Be specific about what is and isn't acceptable when enforcing a boundary. Instead of saying, "Please try to stick to the agreed schedule," say, "I expect you to follow the schedule we've agreed on for the children's handover times. If there's an issue, communicate in advance." Specificity leaves less room for interpretation or excuse-making, which narcissists often exploit.

By adopting these assertive communication techniques, you set a tone of strength and clarity that makes it harder for your ex to manipulate or push your limits. Assertiveness helps you regain power over your emotions and the co-parenting dynamic.

Documenting Violations to Hold Firm in Boundary-Setting

Narcissists often test boundaries to see how far they can push. One of the most effective tools you have in maintaining boundaries is documentation. Keeping records of boundary violations helps you stay aware of patterns and provides tangible evidence should you need to take legal action or involve a third party in the future.

Here's how to document boundary violations effectively:

1. **Keep a Co-Parenting Journal:** Write down every instance where your boundaries were crossed. Include details such as dates, times, the nature of the violation, and any communications (e.g., emails, texts, or phone calls). This doesn't have to be a lengthy process—short, concise entries are enough to maintain a record.

2. **Use Email and Text for Communication:** Whenever possible, communicate in writing. Text messages and emails provide a written record that is harder to dispute than a verbal conversation. If your ex attempts to gaslight or twist events, you'll have clear documentation of the exchange. Tools like co-parenting apps can also be helpful, as they track communication and agreements.

3. **Save Evidence of Manipulation:** Narcissists often operate in subtle ways, testing your boundaries through manipulation or passive-aggressive behavior. For example, they may consistently return the children late or make unreasonable demands about schedule changes. Save all evidence of these behaviors, especially if they impact the children's well-being or your parenting time.

By documenting these violations, you create a buffer between yourself and the chaos the narcissist thrives on. It also helps you stay grounded in reality, preventing the narcissist's attempts to gaslight or confuse you into questioning your own perceptions.

The Importance of Consistency in Enforcing Boundaries

Consistency is the key to maintaining effective boundaries. Boundaries that are only enforced sporadically will not hold up against the persistent pressure of a narcissist. Narcissists are experts at testing the waters to see where they can push, and if they sense any inconsistency, they will exploit it to their advantage.

Here's why consistency is critical and how to ensure you maintain it:

- **Avoid Backsliding:** It can be tempting to relax boundaries in moments of peace or when things seem to be going well. However, this is often when the narcissist is biding their time, waiting for an opportunity to reassert control. By keeping your boundaries firm at all times, you send a clear message that you won't tolerate manipulation, no matter the circumstances.

- **Communicate Consequences:** Consistent enforcement also means that there must be consequences for boundary violations. Communicate these consequences clearly when a boundary is set, and follow through every time. For instance, if your ex continuously changes the schedule without prior agreement, you might say, "If the schedule isn't respected moving forward, I'll be seeking legal intervention to ensure it's enforced."

- **Involve Third Parties When Necessary:** Sometimes, the narcissist will ignore your boundaries entirely, regardless of how assertive or consistent you are. In these cases, involving a third party, such as a mediator, lawyer, or court order, may be necessary to enforce compliance. This is where your documentation becomes crucial, providing evidence of repeated boundary violations and your efforts to maintain consistency.

Consistency requires resilience, especially when dealing with someone who will use every tool at their disposal to break your resolve. But remember: the more consistent you are, the less power the narcissist will have over you, and the more emotionally free you will become.

Case Study: Enforcing Boundaries in a High-Conflict Co-Parenting Relationship

Bethany, a mother of three young children, had recently divorced her narcissistic ex-husband, Mark. Throughout their marriage, Mark had used manipulation, gaslighting, and control tactics to dominate Bethany. After the divorce, Bethany hoped the situation would improve, but Mark continued his controlling behavior through their co-parenting relationship. He regularly disregarded the custody schedule, made last-minute changes, and used the children as pawns to manipulate Bethany.

The Problem: Bethany struggled to enforce boundaries with Mark. Whenever she tried to set limits, Mark would gaslight her, claiming she was being unreasonable or overly controlling. He also attempted to guilt her into changing plans to suit his needs, and when Bethany didn't comply, he would lash out by belittling her parenting in front of the children. This left Bethany emotionally exhausted and questioning her ability to maintain boundaries.

Steps to Solution: Realizing the detrimental effects this was having on both her and her children, Bethany sought help from a therapist who specialized in co-parenting with narcissists. The therapist introduced Bethany to several techniques to enforce boundaries confidently.

1. **Establishing Clear Boundaries:** Bethany identified the areas where boundaries were most necessary: communication, scheduling, and decision-making about the children. She made it clear

that all communication about the children would take place through email, that the custody schedule would be adhered to, and that any changes needed to be discussed in advance. By setting these specific boundaries, Bethany reduced Mark's ability to control the situation through unpredictable behavior.

2. **Using Assertive Communication:** Bethany learned to use "I" statements to express her needs without appearing confrontational. Instead of reacting emotionally to Mark's provocations, she calmly restated her expectations: "I need us to stick to the custody schedule for the children's stability. If changes need to be made, I expect to be notified at least 24 hours in advance." By remaining calm and direct, Bethany minimized the emotional drama that Mark was trying to create.

3. **Documenting Violations:** Bethany began documenting every instance when Mark violated a boundary, including the violation's date, time, and nature. She saved all email and text communications to create a record of his behavior. This documentation helped her stay grounded, allowing her to see the patterns in Mark's manipulation. It also gave her the evidence she needed if she ever needed to take legal action.

4. **Consistent Enforcement of Boundaries:** One of Bethany's most significant changes was staying consistent in enforcing boundaries. In the past, she had given in to Mark's demands in hopes of avoiding conflict. However, Bethany realized that this only empowered Mark to continue his behavior. By enforcing the agreed-upon boundaries every time they were crossed, Bethany gradually weakened Mark's control over her.

5. **Seeking Legal Backup:** When Mark continued to disregard the custody schedule, Bethany sought legal advice. Her lawyer helped her file for a court order that legally enforced the custody arrangement. With the documented violations, Bethany had the evidence she needed to show the court that Mark was not adhering to the agreements. The court order gave Bethany the legal backing to hold Mark accountable for his actions.

The Outcome: Over time, Bethany's consistent boundary enforcement began to change the dynamics of her co-parenting relationship. Mark, who thrived on unpredictability and manipulation, could no longer get the emotional reaction he craved from Bethany. Bethany stayed emotionally detached by using the gray rock method, giving Mark minimal responses and refusing to engage in arguments.

With legal boundaries in place, Mark had no choice but to follow the custody schedule, and any changes required prior agreement. The reduction in conflict had a positive impact on the children as well. They started feeling more secure with the predictability of the custody arrangements, and Bethany noticed they were less anxious during transitions between households.

Key Lessons from the Case Study

- **Assertiveness Reduces Manipulation:** Bethany's shift from reactive to assertive communication helped her maintain control of the co-parenting situation. By using clear, calm language, she minimized opportunities for Mark to provoke her emotionally.

- **Documentation is Power:** Keeping a detailed record of boundary violations provided Bethany with the evidence she needed to protect herself legally and emotionally. This documentation served as an objective reminder of Mark's manipulative behavior, preventing Bethany from second-guessing herself when he tried to gaslight her.

- **Consistency is Key:** Bethany learned that boundaries only work if they are enforced consistently. By maintaining firm boundaries every time they were tested, she gradually diminished Mark's ability to control her, ultimately reducing conflict.

- **Legal Backup Strengthens Boundaries:** When emotional tactics weren't enough, Bethany sought legal intervention. The court order reinforced her boundaries, providing a layer of protection and ensuring that Mark had to respect the custody schedule.

Conclusion: Bethany's experience demonstrates that while co-parenting with a narcissist is challenging, maintaining boundaries with consistency and confidence is possible. Through assertive communication, documentation, emotional detachment, and legal support when necessary, Bethany regained control over her life and created a more stable environment for her children. This case study serves as a powerful example of how clear, consistent boundary enforcement can neutralize the manipulative tactics of a narcissistic co-parent.

Chapter Wrap-up

In this chapter, we explored how to effectively set and enforce boundaries in a high-conflict co-parenting relationship, particularly with a narcissistic ex-partner. We discussed the importance of assertive communication, focusing on "I" statements and maintaining emotional neutrality to avoid escalating conflict. By using clear and direct language, you set a tone that prevents manipulation and keeps interactions focused on the well-being of your children.

We also emphasized the value of documentation. Keeping a record of boundary violations is critical for your emotional clarity and as evidence if legal action becomes necessary. This documentation ensures you remain grounded in reality and not swayed by gaslighting or manipulation.

Consistency is crucial, and the chapter detailed the need for consistent boundary enforcement. Without consistency, boundaries lose their effectiveness, allowing the narcissistic co-parent to test and violate them more easily. Consistently enforcing consequences for boundary violations builds strength over time, reducing the narcissist's control.

With the foundation of boundaries firmly in place, you've taken a critical step toward protecting both yourself and your children from the manipulative tactics of a narcissistic co-parent. But setting boundaries is only part of the journey. In the next chapter, we'll delve into an even more profound aspect of your emotional strength—**Resilience**. Building resilience ensures that you can weather future challenges, recover from setbacks, and continue to protect your emotional well-being, no matter what obstacles arise.

Chapter 11

Resilience: Building Lasting Emotional Strength

"You can't stop the waves, but you can learn to surf."
— *Jon Kabat-Zinn*

In this chapter, we will explore the essence of resilience—how it can transform setbacks into opportunities for growth for you and your children. As a parent navigating the difficult landscape of co-parenting with a narcissistic ex-partner, resilience is one of your most powerful tools. It helps you weather emotional storms, bounce back from adversity, and create a stable, peaceful environment for your family. By embracing resilience, you safeguard your emotional well-being and provide a model of strength and stability for your children. This chapter will guide you through the strategies you need to cultivate long-term emotional strength and maintain peace in the face of ongoing challenges.

Resilience is often misunderstood as a natural trait—something you either have or you don't. However, resilience is more like a muscle you can develop and strengthen over time. This chapter will demystify resilience by offering actionable steps to help you build it within yourself and foster it in your children. You'll learn how to turn setbacks into stepping stones, creating emotional safety and stability for your family that will last long after the immediate challenges of co-parenting have faded. In learning to navigate these difficult circumstances with strength and calm, you empower yourself and teach your children valuable lessons in emotional resilience.

The strategies in this chapter will equip you to bounce back from setbacks, maintain your emotional equilibrium, and ensure that you and your children thrive, no matter your obstacles. Let's delve into the practical steps you can take to cultivate resilience and provide lasting emotional security for your family.

Emotional Regulation for Resilience

At the heart of resilience lies the ability to regulate your emotions effectively. Emotional regulation doesn't mean suppressing your feelings but managing them in a way that allows you to respond thoughtfully rather than react impulsively. When dealing with a narcissistic ex-partner, it can be easy to get swept up in the emotional chaos they often create. However, resilience requires you to maintain emotional stability, even in the face of provocation.

Start by identifying your emotional triggers. What situations or interactions cause you to feel overwhelmed, angry, or frustrated? Once you've identified your triggers, you can begin to anticipate these moments and prepare yourself emotionally. One effective method for doing this is through mindfulness, a practice that helps you stay grounded in the present moment, making it easier to navigate emotionally charged situations calmly and clearly.

Emotional regulation is equally crucial for your children. Children often model their emotional responses on what they see from their parents, which makes your role in teaching them resilience all the more important. Help your children identify their emotions and give them the tools to manage those feelings in healthy ways. Techniques like deep breathing, counting to ten, or even having a "calm down" space can be highly effective in teaching children how to regulate their emotions, setting them up for long-term emotional resilience.

Bouncing Back from Setbacks

Resilience isn't just about avoiding setbacks—it's about learning how to bounce back from them. Life, particularly in the context of co-parenting with a narcissist, is filled with challenges that can make you feel like you're constantly fighting uphill battles. However, each setback can also be viewed as an opportunity for growth. The key is to shift your mindset from one of victimhood to one of empowerment.

When you encounter a setback—a difficult interaction with your ex-partner, an unexpected legal battle, or a parenting challenge—it's essential to allow yourself to feel the emotions that arise. However, don't stay stuck in those emotions. Instead, use them as a launching pad to reassess the situation and find a way to move forward. Ask yourself: What can I learn from this experience? How can I apply this lesson to future challenges? By reframing setbacks as learning opportunities, you begin to build resilience naturally.

For children, setbacks can often feel overwhelming. They may not have the emotional maturity to process complex feelings like disappointment, frustration, or sadness. As a parent, you can help them develop resilience by normalizing these emotions and teaching them that setbacks are a natural part of life. Encourage them to reflect on their experiences and think about what they've learned. This simple act of reflection helps children see that setbacks are temporary and that they have the strength to overcome them.

Practical Strategies for Building Resilience

Resilience doesn't develop overnight. It's a process that requires consistent effort and practice. The following strategies will help you and your children build lasting resilience, ensuring that emotional stability becomes the foundation of your co-parenting journey.

- **Journaling for Reflection:** Writing about your experiences is one of the most effective ways to process emotions and build resilience. Keep a journal to reflect on daily challenges and the emotions they evoke. Encourage your children to do the same, even if it's in a simplified format like drawing or writing down one word that describes how they're feeling.

- **Set Small, Achievable Goals:** Resilience is strengthened through small victories. Set attainable daily or weekly goals, such as maintaining calm during a difficult conversation with your ex or helping your child navigate a stressful situation. Celebrate these wins, no matter how small, as they are building blocks of resilience.

- **Develop a Support Network:** Resilience is not built in isolation. Surround yourself with supportive friends, family, or professional counselors who can offer guidance and encouragement. Having trusted adults outside of the family dynamic can provide stability and emotional security for your children.

- **Teach Problem-Solving Skills:** Resilient people aren't deterred by challenges; they face them head-on. Teach your children problem-solving skills by working through issues together. Whether it's a conflict at school or a disagreement with a friend, guide them in finding solutions rather than focusing on the problem itself.

- **Mindfulness and Meditation:** Incorporating mindfulness or meditation practices into your daily routine can dramatically increase resilience. Even five minutes of focused breathing or quiet reflection can help reset your emotional state, making it easier to handle difficult situations.

- **Model Resilience:** As a parent, you are the most significant influence on your children's emotional development. Model resilience by showing them how you handle stress, disappointment, or setbacks. Let them see that, while you may struggle, you always find a way to move forward.

Creating Emotional Safety for the Family

One of the most important benefits of building resilience is the emotional safety it creates within the family. When you are emotionally resilient, you are better equipped to provide your children with a stable, nurturing environment. They will feel secure knowing that no matter what challenges arise, you are strong enough to handle them. This emotional safety allows your children to grow and thrive, knowing they have a solid foundation to rely on.

Emotional safety also involves setting clear boundaries with your ex-partner. Resilience gives you the strength to maintain those boundaries, even when your ex attempts to violate them. By staying calm and firm, you protect yourself and your children from emotional harm and reinforce the stability you've worked so hard to create.

Case Study: Rebecca's Journey to Building Emotional Resilience

Rebecca, a 38-year-old mother of two, co-parented with her ex-husband, Tom, for nearly three years. Tom exhibited many narcissistic behaviors—he was controlling and manipulative and often escalated conflicts during parenting exchanges. Rebecca, who initially struggled with emotional overwhelm after their divorce, constantly found herself reacting to Tom's provocations, which left her emotionally drained and impacted her ability to parent her children effectively.

Rebecca noticed that her children were becoming anxious during transitions between homes and often mimicked the tense energy she brought back from her interactions with Tom. She realized she needed to regain control over her emotions not only for her well-being but also for the emotional health of her children. This realization pushed her to start working on building resilience.

Challenge: The biggest challenge Rebecca faced was her emotional reactions to Tom's provocations. He would make unreasonable demands, manipulate situations to make her feel guilty, and frequently try to paint her as the "bad parent" to their children. These interactions often triggered strong emotional responses, leaving Rebecca angry, frustrated, and reactive. Her children were also beginning to show signs of stress, becoming withdrawn and anxious during exchanges with their father.

The Turning Point: After a particularly tense argument with Tom that left her emotionally exhausted, Rebecca decided it was time to break the cycle. She sought counseling and began researching ways to build resilience and emotional regulation. She realized that while she couldn't change Tom's behavior, Rebecca could change how she responded. Her goal became to remain emotionally stable, no matter what Tom did or said.

The Solution - Building Resilience: Rebecca implemented several key strategies to build her emotional resilience and help her children do the same:

- **Emotional Regulation through Mindfulness:** Rebecca learned mindfulness techniques to help her manage her emotional triggers. To keep herself grounded, she practiced deep breathing exercises before and after interactions with Tom. She also introduced mindfulness to her children, teaching them to breathe deeply when they felt anxious or overwhelmed.

- **Reframing Setbacks:** Instead of viewing her conflicts with Tom as failures or setbacks, Rebecca began to see them as opportunities to practice her new resilience skills. Each time she remained calm during an interaction, she reflected on her progress. She started journaling her emotions after each challenging situation, which helped her process feelings constructively.

- **Modeling Resilience for Her Children:** Rebecca knew her children were learning to manage emotions by watching her. She consciously modeled resilience by remaining calm during co-parenting exchanges, even when Tom tried to provoke her. She also started having open conversations with her children about feelings, encouraging them to express their emotions without fear.

- **Building a Support Network:** Understanding the importance of having a strong support system, Rebecca reached out to friends and family for help when needed. She also joined a support group for parents dealing with narcissistic ex-partners, which provided her with emotional support and practical advice.

- **Establishing Boundaries:** One of the most significant steps Rebecca took was to develop clear emotional and communication boundaries with Tom. She adopted the Gray Rock Method to emotionally detach from his provocations, responding to his attempts to instigate conflict with neutral, non-emotional replies. This method minimized the emotional impact of their interactions, allowing her to remain focused on her children's well-being.

The Outcome: Within a few months, Rebecca noticed significant changes in her and her children's emotional well-being. She no longer felt emotionally drained after interactions with Tom, and her children appeared more relaxed during parenting exchanges. They started mimicking her calm energy, and their anxiety levels decreased.

Through consistent practice, Rebecca built lasting emotional resilience. She no longer reacted emotionally to Tom's provocations and felt more in control of her emotional responses. As a result, her co-parenting journey became less about conflict and more about creating a stable, peaceful environment for her children.

Key Takeaways:

- **Emotional Regulation:** Rebecca's ability to practice mindfulness allowed her to manage her emotions and avoid reacting to her ex-husband's provocations.

- **Reframing Setbacks:** By viewing difficult interactions as learning opportunities, Rebecca developed resilience and empowered herself to grow from each experience.

- **Modeling Resilience:** Rebecca's calm and emotionally stable responses helped her children develop their emotional resilience.

- **Boundaries and Detachment:** The Gray Rock Method allowed Rebecca to emotionally detach from conflict, maintaining her peace and focusing on her children's well-being.

- **Support Network:** Leaning on her support system gave Rebecca the emotional strength she needed to stay resilient.

Chapter Wrap-up

Resilience is not a one-time achievement—it's a lifelong skill that will continue to serve you and your family as you move forward. The challenges of co-parenting with a narcissist may not disappear, but your ability to handle them with grace and strength will only grow. By consistently practicing the strategies outlined in this chapter, you'll ensure that you and your children are emotionally equipped to face whatever comes your way.

RESILIENCE: BUILDING LASTING EMOTIONAL STRENGTH

The resilience you build today will improve your current situation and set the stage for long-term peace, stability, and emotional health. As you continue to develop this skill, you'll find that setbacks no longer derail you but instead become opportunities for growth, reflection, and renewed strength.

In this chapter, we explored the essential strategies for building lasting emotional resilience for you and your children. Resilience is the ability to bounce back from setbacks and grow stronger through adversity, a critical skill for those navigating the challenges of co-parenting with a narcissist.

Key Points:

- **Emotional Regulation:** The foundation of resilience is learning to manage your emotional responses, rather than reacting impulsively. Mindfulness techniques and identifying emotional triggers are vital for maintaining stability.

- **Setbacks as Growth Opportunities:** Instead of seeing setbacks as failures, they should be reframed as opportunities for growth. This mindset shift is crucial for building emotional strength.

- **Practical Strategies:** Journaling, goal-setting, and building a strong support network are practical ways to strengthen resilience over time. These tools help both parents and children manage challenges effectively.

- **Emotional Safety:** Creating an emotionally safe environment is key to resilience. By establishing clear boundaries and modeling emotional stability, parents can ensure their children thrive in the face of co-parenting difficulties.

Ultimately, this chapter provided you with actionable strategies to foster resilience, ensuring you and your children can navigate co-parenting challenges with strength and emotional stability.

As you've now built a foundation of resilience for both yourself and your children, it's important to remember that co-parenting with a narcissist isn't just about daily routines—it's also about navigating major life events where tensions can run high. Birthdays, holidays, and school events can become emotional battlegrounds if not approached with the right mindset.

In the next chapter, you'll learn strategies to maintain emotional control and minimize conflict while navigating major life events with your narcissistic ex. The resilience you've built will serve as your anchor, enabling you to create positive experiences for your children, even in the face of potential conflict.

Part III: Thriving Beyond Co-Parenting

"People are like stained-glass windows. They sparkle and shine when the sun is out, but when the darkness sets in, their true beauty is revealed only if there is a light from within." – Elisabeth Kübler-Ross

What if co-parenting with a narcissist could be less about survival and more about thriving?

In this part of the book, we move beyond the immediate challenges and emotional hurdles of co-parenting and explore how to truly flourish in a situation that once felt overwhelming. It's about finding peace in the storm and learning to manage your life and your children's well-being while interacting with a difficult ex-partner. This chapter will empower you with strategies that allow you to reclaim not just control but a sense of peace and emotional freedom. The tools and insights shared here are designed to give you the confidence and strength to navigate even the most challenging situations.

By the end of this section, you'll know how to protect your children's emotional health, handle major life events, and keep calm even when your ex tries to escalate conflicts.

Chapter 12

Navigating Major Life Events With Your Narcissistic Ex

"Co-parenting is not a competition between two homes. It is a collaboration of parents doing what is best for the kids." — **Heather Hetchler**

Major life events like birthdays, holidays, and graduations hold immense emotional value, but co-parenting with a narcissistic ex can turn these joyous occasions into minefields. Narcissists often use these events to stir up conflict or steal the spotlight, knowing they hold emotional significance. If you're not prepared, the manipulation can escalate, leaving you and your children feeling frustrated and powerless. But with the right strategies, you can minimize their influence and create positive, lasting memories for your children.

The key to mastering these situations is maintaining emotional control and focusing on what truly matters—your children's well-being. With thoughtful preparation and emotional resilience, you can navigate these high-stakes events without allowing your ex to cause disruption or chaos. In this chapter, we will explore strategies to celebrate these moments with joy and confidence, regardless of your ex-partner's behavior.

Planning for Major Life Events

One of the most powerful tools at your disposal is planning ahead. Preparation is essential when you know your narcissistic ex is likely to try and sabotage an important event. By anticipating their tactics, you can stay one step ahead and maintain control over the situation. Start by creating a structured plan that accounts for potential conflicts. For example, decide on logistics early: who will be invited, where the event will take place, and how responsibilities will be divided.

Set clear boundaries regarding participation. If your ex tends to make scenes at public events, consider limiting their role or even excluding them if it's in the best interest of your children. Communicate these boundaries clearly and stick to them. It's important to involve any legal agreements, such as custody schedules, in your planning to ensure that you are within your rights when setting limits.

- **Designate roles ahead of time:** By assigning specific tasks and responsibilities beforehand, you reduce the opportunity for conflict. For example, if it's a child's birthday party, one parent can handle the cake while the other manages activities. This reduces the chance of spontaneous disagreements.

- **Create a backup plan:** Always have an alternative arrangement ready if your ex refuses to cooperate or shows signs of causing trouble. For example, have a friend or family member on standby to step in if things start to escalate.

- **Focus on the details that matter:** While getting caught up in logistics is tempting, remember that the goal is to create positive memories for your children. Keep the event centered on their happiness, not potential conflicts with your ex.

Managing Emotional Reactions

When emotions run high, it's easy to lose control, especially during events that should be joyful but are disrupted by your ex. Narcissists thrive on creating emotional turmoil, but you can counter this by learning to manage your emotional reactions.

One effective method is mindfulness, which involves being fully present in the moment and observing your thoughts and emotions without reacting impulsively. If your ex tries to provoke you, take a deep breath, ground yourself, and focus on what you can control—your own response.

- **Practice deep breathing techniques:** When you feel your emotions escalating, take a moment to pause and breathe. Deep breathing activates your parasympathetic nervous system, which helps to calm your body's stress response.

- **Visualize a positive outcome:** Before the event, visualize how you want the day to unfold. Imagine yourself staying calm, collected, and focused on your children. This mental preparation can help you stay centered when challenges arise.

- **Have a support system:** Invite a trusted friend or family member to the event who can provide emotional support. Sometimes, just having someone who understands your situation can make all the difference in maintaining composure.

The goal is not to suppress your emotions but to manage them in a way that prevents your ex from gaining control. Remember, narcissists seek to provoke a reaction—don't give them the satisfaction.

Minimizing the Narcissist's Influence

Minimizing your ex's influence is a critical element of navigating major life events. Narcissists will often attempt to hijack important moments, drawing attention away from your children and towards themselves. They may create drama, stir conflict, or act out in ways designed to undermine the event's success.

One of the most effective ways to counter this is by limiting communication. If your ex isn't directly involved in organizing the event, keep communication to a minimum. Use written forms of communication like email or text, where you can maintain a record of all interactions. Avoid verbal confrontations that could escalate emotionally.

- **Use the Gray Rock Method:** This technique involves being as emotionally unresponsive as possible. When your ex tries to provoke you or dominate the conversation, respond in a neutral, non-reactive manner. This reduces their ability to manipulate the situation.

- **Stay focused on the children:** It's easy to get sucked into the narcissist's games, but your priority should always be your children. Keep the focus on them and the joy of the occasion. By directing your attention to what matters, you minimize the narcissist's ability to cause harm.

- **Avoid public confrontations:** Narcissists often thrive on an audience. If you anticipate conflict, choose to resolve disagreements privately and away from the main event. This can help de-escalate potential flare-ups and preserve the overall atmosphere of the occasion.

Creating Positive Experiences for Your Children

While the presence of a narcissistic ex can be draining, your focus should always be on creating positive experiences for your children. You can't control how your ex behaves, but you can control the environment you create for your children during these significant moments.

Encourage your children to focus on the aspects of the event they enjoy, whether it's the games, the food, or simply being surrounded by loved ones. Reinforce that these events are about them, not the conflicts or difficulties between their parents.

- **Celebrate your children's individuality:** Make sure the event reflects their interests and personalities, ensuring they feel valued and seen. This can make the day more meaningful and help them associate these moments with positivity rather than parental conflict.

- **Document the day positively:** Take photos and videos to create lasting memories that emphasize the joy of the event. Later, when your children reflect on the day, they'll remember the love and happiness, not the drama.

- **Debrief after the event:** Once the event is over, talk to your children about how they felt. Use this opportunity to reinforce the positives and address any uncomfortable moments in a way that provides emotional reassurance.

Case Study: Navigating Major Life Events with a Narcissistic Co-Parent

Gina and Bobby divorced two years ago after a tumultuous relationship clouded by Bobby's narcissistic behaviors. They have two children together, 8-year-old Emma and 10-year-old Luke. Gina has primary custody, but they co-parent, meaning Gina and Bobby must interact frequently about school events, holidays, and birthdays. Bobby consistently uses these moments as opportunities to reassert control, often turning significant family events into stressful confrontations.

One of the biggest challenges Gina faced was preparing for Emma's birthday party. Bobby was determined to make himself the center of attention, insisting on being overly involved in the planning and questioning Gina's every decision. He would drop passive-aggressive comments about the guest list and the choice of venue, creating stress and drama in the lead-up to the event.

The Challenge: Gina was committed to making the party a joyful experience for Emma, but Bobby's behavior quickly turned it into a power struggle. He frequently demanded changes to the plans and used emotional manipulation to try to make Gina feel guilty. For example, he insisted on inviting people from his side of the family that Emma had little connection with, arguing that "they have a right to be there" despite Emma's expressed preference for a smaller gathering with close friends.

Gina realized that unless she found a way to manage Bobby's behavior and set firm boundaries, unnecessary conflict would overshadow the event. She knew she needed to protect her daughter's special day from becoming a battleground for Bobby's need for control and validation.

Strategy: To manage the situation and minimize Bobby's disruptive influence, Gina implemented several key strategies:

1. **Limiting Communication:** Gina shifted all planning-related communication to email. This allowed her to create a written record of every interaction, which helped her remain emotionally detached when Bobby's messages turned manipulative or provocative. She refused to engage in phone calls or in-person conversations about the party, knowing that these interactions often escalated into arguments.

2. **Gray Rock Method:** When Bobby attempted to provoke her or make emotional appeals, Gina responded in a neutral and unemotional manner, sticking strictly to the facts. When he suggested uninvited guests, she simply replied, "Emma prefers a smaller party with her close friends," and did not elaborate further. She kept the conversations short and focused by not feeding into his need for attention or validation.

3. **Focusing on the Children:** Gina consciously decided to focus

on Emma's excitement and what would make her day special. She engaged Emma in the party planning, letting her choose the theme and the activities. This helped Emma feel that the day was about her, reinforcing the event's true purpose—celebrating her, not appeasing Bobby.

4. **Creating Backup Plans:** Knowing Bobby's tendency to cause last-minute disruptions, Gina created contingency plans. She had a trusted friend ready to step in if Bobby showed up unannounced or attempted to disrupt the event. She also arranged for a family member to help with party logistics, ensuring she could focus on Emma without being distracted by potential conflicts with Bobby.

5. **Public vs. Private Confrontations:** On the day of the party, Bobby arrived late, visibly irritated that the event had already started. He criticized the arrangements in front of some of the guests, but Gina calmly redirected the conversation. "Today is about Emma and her friends having fun," she said, refusing to let Bobby's comments derail the party. When he tried to bring up another issue later, she suggested they discuss it privately after the event. This approach kept the party focused on Emma and prevented a public scene.

Outcome: By using these strategies, Gina successfully navigated the event with minimal disruption. Emma's birthday party went smoothly, with the children enjoying the games and activities that Gina had thoughtfully planned. Bobby's attempts to undermine the day were largely neutralized by Gina's refusal to engage in emotional conflict.

After the party, Gina took some time to talk with Emma about her experience. Emma's feedback was overwhelmingly positive, and she hardly mentioned her father's behavior, indicating that she had not been affected by his attempts to cause friction. The birthday party had been about Emma and her happiness, just as Gina had intended.

Gina also took the time to reflect on her own emotional responses. She noted that her decision to limit communication and use the Gray Rock Method had allowed her to stay calm and focused, preventing her from being dragged into unnecessary conflicts with Bobby. This success motivated Gina to continue using these strategies in future co-parenting situations.

Key Takeaways

- **Boundaries are Essential:** Limiting communication to email helped Gina maintain emotional distance and provided her with a record of all interactions, which helped her avoid emotional manipulation.

- **Neutral Responses Defuse Conflict:** The Gray Rock Method disarmed Bobby's provocations by preventing him from gaining the emotional response he sought. Keeping her responses neutral and fact-based stopped Bobby from escalating the situation.

- **Focus on the Children:** By involving Emma in the party planning, Gina ensured that the focus stayed on her child's happiness, not the conflict with her ex. Despite her father's behavior, this allowed Emma to have a positive experience.

- **Prepare for Disruptions:** Gina's backup plans—having a trusted friend on standby and maintaining a calm, focused demeanor—allowed her to handle unexpected disruptions without derailing the event.

- **Debriefing Provides Emotional Support:** Talking to Emma after the event reinforced the positive aspects of the day and provided an opportunity to discuss any difficult moments, offering emotional reassurance to Emma.

Conclusion: Navigating major life events with a narcissistic co-parent can be challenging. Still, with the right strategies in place, it is possible to minimize their influence and create positive experiences for your children. By focusing on boundaries, emotional regulation, and planning, Gina protected her daughter's birthday from becoming a conflict zone, ensuring that the day was about joy and celebration.

Chapter Wrap-up

In this chapter, we explored strategies to help you manage major life events like birthdays, holidays, and graduations while co-parenting with a narcissistic ex. The focus is on minimizing the narcissist's disruptive influence, protecting your children's experiences, and maintaining your emotional control throughout these high-stakes situations. Here are the key takeaways:

1. **Limit Communication:** Use written communication, like email or text, to document interactions and avoid unnecessary emotional engagement. This helps you maintain control and create a clear record of all discussions.

2. **Gray Rock Method:** Respond to provocations in a neutral, un-

emotional way to avoid feeding into the narcissist's need for attention. This technique reduces their ability to escalate the situation and helps you stay calm.

3. **Stay Focused on Your Children:** Keep the spotlight on your children's happiness and experiences. Redirect attention away from the narcissist and focus on creating positive memories for your children during these events.

4. **Avoid Public Confrontations:** Narcissists often thrive on an audience. Handle conflicts privately and calmly to prevent public arguments that could ruin the atmosphere. Use de-escalation techniques to keep the peace.

5. **Prepare Backup Plans:** Have trusted friends or family on standby to help manage unexpected disruptions. Creating contingency plans ensures that you're ready for your ex's attempts to cause chaos.

With the right strategies, handling major life events with your narcissistic ex can become less about conflict and more about celebrating the things that truly matter—your children's happiness and well-being. By planning ahead, managing your emotions, and keeping the focus on your children, you can ensure these important milestones remain joyful and conflict-free.

As you master these techniques, it's time to focus on an even greater challenge: helping your children build emotional resilience in the face of narcissistic behavior. In the next chapter, we will explore strategies to teach your children how to navigate their relationship with the narcissistic parent, ensuring they grow up emotionally strong and resilient.

Chapter 13

Helping Your Children Build Emotional Resilience

"You are braver than you believe, stronger than you seem, and smarter than you think." — A.A. Milne (Winnie the Pooh)

Emotional resilience is a fundamental life skill that encompasses adapting to stressful situations and recovering from adversity. Not merely about enduring hardship, it involves actively engaging with one's emotions and employing effective coping strategies to navigate life's challenges. Developing emotional resilience is vital for children as it lays the foundation for their mental health and overall well-being.

The Importance of Emotional Resilience

Children equipped with emotional resilience are better prepared to face various emotional upheavals throughout their lives. This capacity is particularly crucial when dealing with a narcissistic co-parent, who may exploit emotional vulnerabilities to exert control. Narcissistic individuals often thrive on creating chaos, manipulation, and emotional turbulence, making it essential for children to possess the tools needed to navigate these complex dynamics.

- **Adapting to Change:** Emotional resilience enables children to adapt to changing circumstances. Resilient children can pivot and adjust their behavior and expectations when facing new environments, social challenges, or family disruptions, reducing anxiety and stress.

- **Managing Stress:** Resilient children have a toolkit of strategies for managing stress effectively. They can employ techniques such as deep breathing, mindfulness, and cognitive reframing to mitigate overwhelming feelings, helping them maintain emotional balance even in tumultuous situations.

- **Enhancing Problem-Solving Skills:** With emotional resilience comes improved problem-solving abilities. Children learn to approach challenges constructively, breaking down problems into manageable parts and exploring multiple solutions. This proactive approach fosters confidence in their ability to handle adversity.

- **Building Stronger Relationships:** Emotional resilience contributes to healthier interpersonal relationships. Children who can regulate their emotions and respond to conflicts calmly are better equipped to communicate effectively and empathize with others, leading to more meaningful connections with peers and family members.

- **Fostering a Positive Outlook:** Resilient children tend to be more optimistic. They can recognize setbacks as temporary and see failures as opportunities for learning and growth, which helps build a sense of hope and perseverance.

Recognizing Signs of Emotional Resilience

While emotional resilience is a developmental process that varies from child to child, several indicators can help parents identify resilient traits:

- **Emotional Awareness:** Children who can articulate their feelings and recognize the emotions of others often exhibit emotional resilience. This self-awareness allows them to navigate their emotional landscape effectively.

- **Persistence in the Face of Challenges:** Resilient children demonstrate determination when encountering obstacles. Rather than giving up easily, they are willing to try again and explore alternative paths to achieve their goals.

- **Adaptive Coping Strategies:** When faced with stress, resilient children are more likely to use positive coping mechanisms, such as seeking support from trusted adults or engaging in physical activities to release pent-up energy.

- **Ability to Regulate Emotions:** Children who can manage their emotional responses to challenging situations—whether through calming techniques or seeking distraction—exhibit a high level of emotional resilience.

The Role of Parents in Fostering Emotional Resilience

Parents play a pivotal role in nurturing their children's emotional resilience. By modeling healthy emotional behaviors and providing support, parents can create a safe environment where children can develop these crucial skills. Here are five ways parents can foster emotional resilience:

1. **Encourage Open Communication:** Create a safe space for your children to express their feelings without judgment. Encourage them to share their thoughts and emotions regularly, reinforcing that talking about their struggles is okay.

2. **Teach Coping Strategies:** Introduce various coping strategies to help children manage stress. These might include deep breathing exercises, visualization techniques, or creative activities. Provide opportunities for them to practice these techniques regularly.

3. **Model Resilience:** Children learn by observing their parents. Demonstrate resilience in your own life by showing how you handle stress, setbacks, and adversity. Share your experiences and coping strategies to reinforce that resilience is a learned behavior.

4. **Encourage Problem-Solving:** When children face challenges, guide them in brainstorming potential solutions. Encourage them to think critically and evaluate the outcomes of different approaches, fostering independence in problem-solving.

5. **Celebrate Efforts and Progress:** Acknowledge your children's efforts, regardless of the outcome. Celebrating their persistence reinforces the idea that resilience is about the journey, not just the destination.

Understanding emotional resilience is essential for parents aiming to help their children navigate the complexities of life, particularly in challenging situations like co-parenting with a narcissist. By fostering this vital skill, parents equip their children with the tools necessary to adapt, thrive, and build a foundation for emotional well-being that will serve them throughout their lives. As children learn to bounce back from adversity, they become more resilient individuals and more compassionate and empathetic members of society.

Resources for Supporting Children's Emotional Resilience

As a parent, having a range of resources at your disposal is crucial for helping your children develop emotional resilience. These tools can empower them to understand their emotions, cope with challenges, and thrive in various situations. Below are some effective resources to consider:

Books and Articles

Providing children with age-appropriate literature is a powerful way to introduce concepts of emotional health and resilience. Books can serve as both educational tools and conversation starters. Here are some recommended titles:

- **"The Color Monster: A Pop-Up Book of Feelings" by Anna Llenas:** This vibrant book uses colors to represent different emotions, helping younger children identify and articulate their feelings in a fun and engaging way. The interactive pop-ups encourage discussions about emotional experiences.

- **"My Many Colored Days" by Dr. Seuss:** In this delightful story, Dr. Seuss describes various emotions through colors and animals, allowing children to connect feelings with visual representations. It's a great resource for teaching emotional vocabulary.

- **"Feelings" by Aliki:** This picture book provides simple explanations of different emotions, making it suitable for preschool and early elementary-age children. It encourages kids to recognize and discuss their feelings in a straightforward manner.

- **"The Invisible String" by Patrice Karst:** This comforting story addresses feelings of separation and loss, showing children that love and connection persist even when they are apart from loved ones. It can be especially helpful for children coping with the emotional upheaval of divorce or separation.

- **"The Whole-Brain Child" by Daniel J. Siegel and Tina Payne Bryson:** This book, aimed at parents, offers insights into how a child's brain develops and how parents can foster emotional intelligence through everyday interactions. It includes practical strategies for nurturing emotional growth.

- **"What to Do When You Worry Too Much" by Dawn Huebner:** This interactive self-help guide teaches children strategies to manage anxiety and worry. It offers practical exercises that parents can do together with their children.

Encouraging your children to read these books or reading together as a family can spark meaningful conversations about feelings and coping strategies, reinforcing their emotional vocabulary.

Workshops and Therapy

Enrolling your child in workshops focused on emotional intelligence or seeking professional guidance can significantly bolster their emotional resilience. Here are some options:

- **Emotional Intelligence Workshops:** Many community centers and educational institutions offer workshops that teach children about emotions, empathy, and social skills. These workshops often include interactive activities that make learning fun and engaging.

- **Mindfulness and Stress Reduction Classes:** Look for local classes or online programs that teach mindfulness practices tailored for children. These classes can help children develop skills in emotional regulation, focus, and stress management.

- **Counseling or Therapy:** If your child struggles with emotional challenges, speaking with a child psychologist or counselor can be beneficial. A professional can provide tailored strategies and support to help your child navigate their feelings effectively.

- **Parent-Child Workshops:** Some organizations offer workshops for parents and children to attend together. These sessions can foster bonding while teaching valuable emotional regulation techniques in a supportive environment.

Educational Apps

In the digital age, educational apps can be excellent tools for teaching emotional regulation skills engagingly and interactively. Here are some recommended apps:

- **"Breathe, Think, Do with Sesame":** This app introduces children to emotional regulation through interactive activities. Kids can help a character manage various situations by practicing deep breathing and problem-solving skills, making learning about emotions fun.

- **"Headspace for Kids"**: A child-friendly version of the popular meditation app, Headspace for Kids offers guided meditations tailored for different age groups. These meditations can help children learn mindfulness techniques that promote emotional calmness and resilience.

- **"Smiling Mind"**: This app offers mindfulness programs specifically designed for children and adolescents. The guided practices help users develop emotional regulation, focus, and relaxation skills, making it a valuable resource for building resilience.

- **"Mood Meter"**: Developed by the Yale Center for Emotional Intelligence, this app helps children identify and articulate their emotions using a color-coded scale. It encourages kids to check in with their feelings throughout the day and promotes discussions about emotional awareness.

- **"Daniel Tiger's Grr-ific Feelings"**: Based on the beloved children's show, this app allows kids to explore feelings through interactive games and videos. It reinforces lessons about empathy, sharing, and understanding emotions in a playful and relatable manner.

Online Resources and Communities

In addition to books and apps, online resources can provide valuable support for parents and children:

- **Websites:** Many organizations dedicated to child development and mental health offer free resources, articles, and activity ideas for fostering emotional resilience. Websites like the Child Mind Institute and the American Psychological Association provide evidence-based information on child psychology and emotional well-being.

- **Online Forums:** Consider joining online parenting communities or forums where you can share experiences, seek advice, and gain support from other parents facing similar challenges. Platforms like Reddit or parenting groups on Facebook can provide a sense of camaraderie and shared learning.

- **Podcasts:** Look for parenting podcasts focusing on emotional intelligence and child development. Listening to experts discuss strategies and experiences can offer fresh insights and motivate you to implement new practices at home.

Building Resilience Through Activities

Engaging in activities that foster resilience can significantly benefit children by equipping them with essential life skills and enhancing their emotional well-being. Resilience is not only about bouncing back from adversity; it also involves building a foundation of skills that allow children to navigate challenges more effectively. Here are several activities that can help promote resilience in children:

Sports and Physical Activities

Encouraging participation in sports and physical activities is one of the most effective ways to foster resilience. Here's how sports can contribute to emotional growth:

- **Teamwork and Collaboration:** Engaging in team sports teaches children the value of working together towards a common goal. They learn to communicate, cooperate, and support their teammates, which can enhance their social skills and sense of belonging.

- **Perseverance and Goal Setting:** Sports often involve personal and team goals, whether improving a skill or winning a match. Children learn that achieving these goals requires persistence and hard work, helping them understand that success often comes after facing challenges.

- **Stress Relief:** Physical activities are excellent outlets for stress and anxiety. Exercise releases endorphins, which improve mood and reduce feelings of tension. Encouraging regular participation in sports can help children manage their emotions more effectively.

- **Handling Wins and Losses:** Sports provide a natural environment for children to experience victory and defeat. Learning to celebrate achievements while gracefully accepting losses fosters resilience, as they understand that setbacks are a part of life.

- **Developing Discipline:** Regular practice and commitment to a sport instill discipline and routine in children. This structure can help them develop a strong work ethic, essential for overcoming challenges in various aspects of life.

Encouraging children to join local sports teams, participate in community leagues, or even engage in individual sports like swimming or martial arts can significantly contribute to their resilience.

Creative Outlets

Art, music, and drama are powerful tools for emotional expression and can play a vital role in building resilience. Here's how creative activities contribute to emotional growth:

- **Expression of Emotions:** Creative outlets allow children to express their feelings safely and constructively. Whether through painting, writing, or playing music, these activities allow kids to explore and articulate their emotions.

- **Exploration of Identity:** Engaging in creative pursuits helps children discover their interests and passions. This exploration fosters a sense of identity and self-worth, crucial for building resilience.

- **Problem-Solving Skills:** Artistic endeavors often involve experimentation and problem-solving. Children learn to think critically and find innovative solutions, which enhances their ability to adapt to new challenges in other areas of their lives.

- **Coping Mechanism:** Creative activities can serve as effective coping mechanisms during stressful times. Drawing, writing, or playing an instrument can help children process their feelings, reducing anxiety and promoting emotional clarity.

- **Building Confidence:** Completing a creative project or performing in front of an audience can boost a child's self-esteem. This sense of accomplishment reinforces their ability to tackle new challenges, contributing to their resilience.

Encourage your children to explore various creative outlets, whether joining an art class, participating in school plays, or taking music lessons. Provide them with the necessary materials and time to experiment with different forms of expression.

Volunteering

Volunteering offers children unique opportunities to develop empathy, social responsibility, and a sense of purpose, all essential to resilience. Here's how volunteering can benefit children:

- **Instilling Empathy:** Volunteering exposes children to diverse perspectives and experiences. By helping others, they learn to understand and empathize with those facing different challenges, fostering compassion and emotional intelligence.

- **Sense of Purpose:** Volunteer work gives children a sense of contribution and purpose. Knowing their efforts can positively impact others' lives enhances their self-worth and motivates them to continue making a difference.

- **Building Social Skills:** Volunteering often involves teamwork and collaboration with peers or community members. This interaction helps children improve their communication and interpersonal skills, making them more adept at building relationships.

- **Resilience in the Face of Challenges:** Volunteer work can expose children to difficult situations, teaching them how to navigate adversity while maintaining a positive outlook. They learn to appreciate their own circumstances and develop a greater sense of gratitude.

- **Creating Lasting Memories:** Volunteering experiences can create powerful memories and stories that children carry throughout their lives. These experiences contribute to personal growth and strengthen their connection to their community.

To facilitate volunteering opportunities, parents can research local charities, community service organizations, or events where children can get involved. Whether helping at an animal shelter, participating in clean-up drives, or assisting in community kitchens, volunteering is a meaningful way for children to cultivate resilience.

Engaging children in sports, creative activities, and volunteering can significantly enhance their emotional resilience. By participating in these activities, children develop important life skills and gain the tools necessary to cope with challenges and navigate their emotions effectively. As parents, fostering these experiences can provide a supportive environment that nurtures their children's growth, empowering them to face adversity with confidence and strength.

Preparing for Difficult Conversations

Navigating conversations about a narcissistic parent can be incredibly challenging for children, often leaving them feeling confused, anxious, or even guilty. As a supportive parent, preparing for these discussions thoughtfully and constructively is essential. Here are strategies to facilitate these conversations while ensuring your child feels safe and understood.

Use Age-Appropriate Language

One of the most critical aspects of discussing complex topics like narcissism with children is to tailor your language to their developmental level.

- **For Younger Children:** Focus on expressing feelings and behaviors rather than delving into psychological concepts. Use simple, relatable language that connects to their emotions. For instance, you might say, "Sometimes, people can be very focused on what they want, and they might not think about how their actions make others feel." This approach allows younger children to understand the behavior without being overwhelmed by complex terminology.

- **For Older Children and Teenagers:** You can introduce more nuanced discussions about narcissism, as they are likely to have a better grasp of emotional and psychological concepts. Explain how narcissistic behavior can impact relationships and feelings. Use familiar terms but still frame the conversation around their feelings and experiences.

- **Encourage Emotional Literacy:** Regardless of age, help your child develop a vocabulary for discussing their emotions. Teach them words like "frustrated," "disappointed," or "betrayed" so they can articulate their feelings more clearly when talking about their experiences.

Reinforce Their Feelings

Validation is a powerful tool when talking to children about their emotions, especially regarding their experiences with a narcissistic parent.

- **Acknowledge Their Emotions:** Let your child know their feelings are valid and understandable. Use phrases like, "It's okay to feel sad or angry about what happened" or "Many kids feel confused when dealing with these kinds of situations." By normalizing their feelings, you help reduce any guilt or shame they might feel.

- **Provide Emotional Support:** Create a safe space for your child to express their feelings. Encourage them to share what's on their mind and be an active listener. Sometimes, simply being there and showing that you care can make a significant difference.

- **Discuss Common Reactions:** Help them understand that many children in similar situations experience various emotions, including sadness, anger, and confusion. This can reassure them that they are not alone and that their feelings are part of a normal response to a challenging situation.

- **Use Real-Life Examples:** Share stories or examples (keeping their confidentiality and comfort in mind) of how others have felt in similar situations and how they coped. This can help your child feel understood and provide a model for processing their emotions.

Encourage Questions

Creating an open dialogue about their narcissistic parent is essential for your child's emotional health. Here's how to foster an environment that encourages questions:

- **Create a Safe Space for Inquiry:** Assure your child that they can ask anything without fear of judgment. Phrases like, "You can ask me anything, and I'll do my best to help you understand," encourage them to voice their curiosities or concerns.

- **Be Prepared for Tough Questions:** Children may ask difficult questions, such as "Why do they act this way?" or "Is it my fault?" It's crucial to answer honestly, keeping your responses age-appropriate and focused on emotions rather than delving too deep into the complexities of narcissism. For example, you could say, "Some people have a hard time thinking about how their actions affect others, and that can be really hard to understand."

- **Encourage Open-Ended Questions:** Guide your child to express their thoughts by asking them open-ended questions, such as "How does that make you feel?" or "What do you wish was different?" This technique encourages them to explore their feelings more deeply and fosters a greater understanding of their emotional landscape.

- **Follow Up Regularly:** Make discussions about their feelings a regular part of your interactions. Check-in with them about their experiences and emotions, showing them that it's always okay to talk about their feelings and that they don't need to keep everything bottled up inside.

Offer Support and Guidance

In addition to the above strategies, providing ongoing support and guidance is essential in helping your child navigate their feelings about their narcissistic parent.

- **Reinforce Boundaries:** Help your child understand the importance of setting boundaries with their narcissistic parent. Discuss healthy boundaries and empower them to communicate these boundaries assertively.

- **Teach Coping Strategies:** Equip your child with coping strategies to manage their emotions when dealing with their narcissistic parent. Techniques such as deep breathing, journaling, or talking to a trusted adult can give them the tools they need to process their feelings.

- **Encourage Professional Support:** If the emotional burden becomes too heavy for your child, consider seeking help from a child therapist or counselor specializing in family dynamics and emotional resilience. Professional support can offer a safe space for your child to explore their feelings and develop healthy coping mechanisms.

Navigating conversations about a narcissistic parent requires sensitivity, understanding, and patience. By using age-appropriate language, reinforcing their feelings, and encouraging questions, you can create a supportive environment where your child feels safe to express their emotions. Through open dialogue and ongoing support, you empower your child to process their experiences constructively, fostering resilience and emotional strength in challenging familial dynamics.

Case Study: Empowering Children Through Emotional Regulation Techniques

In this case study, we explore the journey of the Thompson family, where Trinity, a 10-year-old girl, navigates the complexities of co-parenting with a narcissistic father. Her mother, Lisa, is determined to provide Trinity with the emotional tools necessary to thrive despite the challenges posed by her father's manipulative behavior.

The Challenge: Trinity often felt anxious and confused after visits with her father. His tendency to dismiss her feelings and focus on his own needs left her feeling emotionally drained. As a result, she struggled with expressing her emotions, often resorting to withdrawal or outbursts when overwhelmed.

Lisa recognized the impact her ex-husband's behavior had on Trinity's emotional health and decided to take proactive steps to equip her daughter with emotional regulation techniques.

Identifying Emotions:

- Lisa introduced Trinity to an Emotion Wheel, a visual tool that helps children identify and articulate their feelings. Together, they would review the wheel after visits with her father to discuss what emotions Trinity experienced during their time together.

- **Outcome:** Trinity became more adept at identifying her feelings, which helped her articulate her experiences more clearly. This awareness empowered her to express her emotions rather than suppress them.

Coping Strategies:

- Lisa taught Trinity several coping strategies, including deep breathing exercises and mindfulness practices. They practiced these techniques together daily, reinforcing their use when Trinity felt overwhelmed.

- **Outcome:** After implementing these strategies, Trinity reported feeling calmer during stressful situations, including interactions with her father. The techniques allowed her to manage her anxiety more effectively.

Open Communication:

- Lisa established a routine of weekly check-ins where they could openly discuss Trinity's feelings. During these sessions, Trinity was encouraged to share her experiences without fear of judgment.

- **Outcome:** Trinity began to open up about her feelings more frequently. She felt validated and understood, knowing her mother was there to support her unconditionally. This created a strong bond between them and fostered an environment of trust.

Creative Expression:

- To help Trinity process her emotions creatively, Lisa encouraged her to engage in art projects and journaling. They set aside time each week for Trinity to create art representing her feelings or write in her journal about her experiences.

- **Outcome:** This creative outlet became a significant tool for Trinity. She found joy in expressing herself artistically and gained insights into her emotional landscape through journaling. The process helped her release pent-up feelings and provided clarity.

Building Resilience through Challenges:

- Lisa encouraged Trinity to participate in team sports, which would help her develop resilience through facing challenges. Trinity joined a local soccer team, where she learned teamwork and perseverance while enjoying physical activity.

- **Outcome:** Engaging in sports boosted Trinity's confidence and provided her with a supportive community. She learned how to cope with wins and losses, reinforcing that setbacks are a part of growth.

Results

Over six months, Trinity showed significant improvement in her emotional well-being:

- **Increased Emotional Awareness:** Trinity became more articulate about her feelings and better understood the triggers for her emotions. She reported feeling less confused and anxious after visits with her father.

- **Enhanced Coping Skills:** With the coping strategies in place, Trinity effectively managed her anxiety and was able to remain calm during difficult interactions with her father.

- **Strengthened Parent-Child Relationship:** The open communication fostered a deeper bond between Trinity and Lisa. Trinity felt more comfortable sharing her experiences, knowing her mother would support her.

- **Development of Resilience:** Participation in sports and creative outlets helped Trinity build resilience, allowing her to approach challenges with a positive mindset. She learned that setbacks are opportunities for growth.

The Thompson family's journey illustrates the profound impact of equipping children with emotional regulation techniques. By fostering emotional awareness, providing coping strategies, and encouraging open communication, Lisa empowered Trinity to navigate the complexities of co-parenting with a narcissistic parent. As a result, Trinity emerged with a healthier emotional outlook and was better equipped to face life's challenges.

This case study is a testament to the effectiveness of emotional regulation techniques in promoting resilience. These techniques ultimately lead to a more nurturing and supportive environment for children facing difficult familial dynamics.

Chapter Wrap-up

This chapter has laid the foundation for your children's emotional health, illustrating how vital emotional regulation techniques are in creating a supportive environment. However, as you continue this journey toward effective co-parenting, it's important to focus on your well-being as well.

The next chapter will explore strategies to help you preserve your emotional stability amid ongoing challenges. You will learn how to establish and maintain boundaries with your narcissistic ex-partner while ensuring that your home remains a sanctuary for you and your children.

Equipping yourself and your children with the right tools and strategies can create a nurturing space where everyone can thrive, even in the face of adversity. Let's delve into how to maintain that essential peace as we move forward together.

Chapter 14

Maintaining Your Peace When Your Ex Tries to Escalate

"Peace is not the absence of conflict, but the ability to cope with it." — Mahatma Gandhi

When dealing with a narcissistic ex-partner, the journey toward peace often triggers an unexpected backlash. Narcissists thrive on control and conflict, and as you begin to regain your emotional footing and establish firm boundaries, they may escalate their attempts to provoke you. In these moments—when their manipulations grow louder, more aggressive, and more desperate—maintaining your peace becomes not just a challenge but a necessity. This chapter aims to prepare you for those escalation attempts and equip you with the tools to stay calm and in control.

Your quiet resilience will give you the strength to handle any attempt to destabilize your newfound peace.

Understanding Escalation Tactics

A narcissist often senses when they're losing their grip on the situation. In response, they escalate their behavior in hopes of reasserting control. Understanding the tactics they use will give you the upper hand. Escalation doesn't always mean shouting matches or confrontations; it can come in subtle, manipulative ways designed to provoke emotional reactions. Here are common tactics narcissists use:

1. **Guilt-tripping and emotional manipulation:** Narcissists know how to play on your emotions, using guilt as a tool to drag you back into the cycle of conflict. They may say things like, "You're abandoning the children," or "You've always been selfish."

2. **Playing the victim:** One of the most manipulative tactics is when the narcissist paints themselves as the victim, accusing you of cruelty or unfairness. This tactic makes you question your actions and feel responsible for their emotional outbursts.

3. **Triangulation:** Narcissists often bring third parties into the conflict to escalate tensions. This could be mutual friends, family members, or even your children. They'll use these people to relay messages or shift blame, forcing you into the middle of unnecessary drama.

4. **Sudden kindness:** Known as "love-bombing," this tactic is particularly insidious. When the narcissist senses you are detaching,

they may temporarily shift tactics, showering you with compliments or affection. This sudden kindness is meant to pull you back in emotionally, only for them to revert to manipulative behaviors once they feel they've regained control.

Understanding these tactics is the first step to preventing them from affecting your peace. The key to success is recognizing them for what they are—manipulations designed to provoke an emotional reaction—and not allowing yourself to get drawn into the conflict.

Strategies for Maintaining Peace

Knowing the tactics is only half the battle. Maintaining peace requires a conscious effort to stay grounded, even when provoked. Here are actionable strategies you can implement when facing escalation attempts from your ex-partner:

Practice Emotional Detachment. Emotional detachment is not the same as disengagement. Detachment means that while you may need to interact with your ex for co-parenting, you don't allow yourself to become emotionally entangled in their provocations. As previously discussed, the Gray Rock Method is an effective method for emotional detachment, as it reduces their motivation to engage because they no longer get the desired reaction.

Maintain Clear, Consistent Boundaries. Establishing boundaries with a narcissist is critical, but maintaining them is the real challenge. The narcissist will test your limits, often trying to break down your boundaries through manipulation or outright aggression. Be firm and clear in your communication. For example, if your boundary is that all communication about the children happens via text, do not engage in phone calls or in-person discussions outside this rule. If the boundary is crossed, calmly remind them of the rule and end the interaction if necessary.

- **Limit Your Responses:** The narcissist thrives on long, drawn-out arguments. Keep your responses brief and factual. For example, if they send you a long, accusatory message, you can respond, "I will be at the school for pickup at 3 PM." Keeping it strictly to the facts and avoiding emotional engagement disempowers their ability to provoke you.

- **Take a Pause Before Reacting:** When provoked, our first instinct is often to defend ourselves or retaliate. However, this only fuels the narcissist's need for conflict. Instead, practice pausing before responding to any escalation attempt. This could be as simple as taking a deep breath, counting to ten, or waiting 24 hours before replying to a message. This not only prevents you from reacting impulsively but also shows the narcissist that their provocations will not trigger a response.

- **Focus on Your Children's Well-Being:** When escalation occurs, it's easy to lose sight of what truly matters: your children. Focusing on their well-being and maintaining a peaceful environment for them will help you navigate these challenges. Remember, by staying calm and maintaining boundaries, you are teaching your children emotional resilience and showing them what healthy responses look like.

Preventing Conflict Re-engagement

One of the hardest parts of maintaining your peace is not getting drawn back into conflict. Narcissists are adept at pushing buttons and creating scenarios where you feel compelled to defend yourself. However, there are strategies that will help you avoid re-engaging in unnecessary conflict:

- **Avoid Justifying Yourself:** Narcissists will often make baseless accusations to provoke a defensive response. They want you to justify your actions because it gives them a sense of control. The best way to disarm this tactic is to refuse to justify yourself. Keep your responses factual and avoid explaining your motives or reasoning.

- **Stick to the Issue at Hand:** When narcissists escalate, they often introduce unrelated issues to confuse and overwhelm you. Stay focused on the core issue and refuse to engage in discussions outside of what is necessary. If the conversation veers off-topic, redirect it back to the point or end the discussion.

- **Use "BIFF" Communication:** Developed by Bill Eddy, the BIFF response method stands for Brief, Informative, Friendly, and Firm. It is a great tool when dealing with a narcissistic ex-partner. Keeping your messages brief, informative, friendly, and firm limits the narcissist's ability to create conflict from your words.

Building Long-Term Resilience

Over time, consistently applying these strategies will not only help you maintain peace but will also build emotional resilience. You'll find that the narcissist's attempts to escalate become less and less impactful as you develop a deeper sense of control over your emotional responses. Here's how to ensure lasting resilience:

- **Self-Care is Non-Negotiable:** Regular self-care is vital to maintaining emotional strength. This could include mindfulness practices, physical exercise, or simply spending time doing activities that bring you joy. Self-care replenishes your emotional reserves, making it harder for the narcissist to provoke you.

- **Surround Yourself with Support:** Having a strong support system is essential. Whether it's friends, family, or a therapist, having people to turn to when things get tough will keep you grounded. Support systems provide a healthy outlet for your emotions and remind you that you're not alone in this journey.

- **Celebrate Small Wins:** It's easy to overlook your progress, especially when the narcissist continues to escalate. But each time you successfully maintain your peace, set a boundary, or refuse to be drawn into conflict, that's a victory. Celebrate these small wins to reinforce your sense of control and resilience.

By mastering these techniques, you will be prepared for any escalation attempts and will find yourself growing stronger, not weaker, in the face of your narcissistic ex's provocations. Each step you take towards maintaining your peace and enforcing your boundaries disempowers their manipulative tactics and strengthens your emotional fortitude.

Case Study: Maintaining Your Peace When Your Ex Tries to Escalate

Kerry, a 38-year-old mother of two, had been co-parenting with her narcissistic ex-husband, David, for over a year since their divorce. Initially, every interaction with David turned into a stressful confrontation, leaving Kerry emotionally drained. Whenever Kerry tried to set boundaries, David would escalate the situation, using guilt-tripping, manipulation, and sometimes involving their children in the conflict. However, with emotional detachment strategies and the E.M.P.O.W.E.R. System guidance, Kerry learned how to maintain her peace, even in the most difficult moments.

The Escalation Tactics Used by David

David escalated his tactics as Kerry grew stronger and more assertive in enforcing her boundaries. He commonly used the following strategies:

- **Guilt-Tripping:** David would say things like, "You're damaging the children by refusing to speak to me" or "If you cared about our family, you'd listen to what I have to say." These statements were meant to make Kerry feel guilty and draw her back into emotional arguments.

- **Playing the Victim:** David often portrayed himself as the one being wronged, telling mutual friends and family that Kerry was "too cold" and "withholding" communication. This triangulation pressured Kerry to justify herself to others.

- **Sudden Kindness (Love-Bombing):** David would switch tactics by being unusually kind after periods of conflict. He would offer to help with the kids or suggest co-parenting meetings, seemingly to work things out. Kerry was initially caught off guard by these shifts and would soften her boundaries, only for David to revert back to manipulative behavior shortly after.

How Kerry Maintained Her Peace

- **Recognizing the Escalation Tactics:** With time, Kerry learned to recognize David's escalation patterns for what they were: manipulative attempts to regain control. Understanding that his provocations were not personal but rather a way to destabilize her was a key turning point for Kerry. She stopped taking his words to heart and began seeing them as part of a predictable pattern of behavior.

- **Using the Gray Rock Method:** Kerry implemented this during interactions with David. For example, when David tried to bait her with emotional accusations, Kerry responded calmly and minimally: "I will be at the school to pick up the children at 3 PM." She avoided engaging in arguments or offering any personal reactions, which eventually reduced David's attempts to provoke her, as he wasn't getting the emotional response he craved.

- **Enforcing Boundaries Consistently:** Kerry was firm with her boundaries. She insisted that all communication be through text unless absolutely necessary. When David tried to discuss personal matters or emotional grievances during child exchanges, Kerry redirected him back to the set boundary, repeating her rules without engaging emotionally. Over time, this consistency reduced the frequency of David's boundary violations.

- **Limiting Her Responses:** Kerry learned to keep her responses to David short, informative, and unemotional. She avoided explaining or justifying herself, which helped her maintain peace. For instance, when David tried to pull her into a debate about holiday arrangements, Kerry simply stated the facts: "The children will be with you from 10 AM to 4 PM as per the custody agreement." By refusing to engage in drawn-out conversations, she minimized opportunities for conflict.

- **Focusing on Her Children's Well-Being:** Through the escalation, Kerry reminded herself that her ultimate goal was to provide a peaceful environment for her children. Whenever she felt the urge to defend herself or react to David's provocations, she focused on the long-term emotional well-being of her children. By maintaining her calm, she modeled emotional regulation for them and created a stable home environment despite the external conflict.

Results and Outcomes

Within six months, Kerry noticed a significant improvement in her interactions with David. His escalation attempts became less frequent and intense as he realized his tactics no longer had the desired effect. Kerry's consistency in enforcing boundaries and refusing to engage emotionally maintained her peace and empowered her children, who felt more secure in a conflict-free environment.

Additionally, Kerry's emotional resilience grew. She no longer dreaded interactions with David because she had developed the tools and strategies to navigate them with calm and control. By staying grounded and refusing to be drawn into conflict, Kerry regained her power and established a peaceful co-parenting dynamic despite David's attempts to escalate.

Key Takeaways from Kerry's Case Study:

- **Recognizing patterns of manipulation is crucial.** Once you understand the escalation tactics, you can disarm them before they take hold.

- **Emotional detachment** through methods like the Gray Rock Method helps prevent emotional reactions and keeps interactions neutral.

- **Consistent boundaries protect your emotional health** and discourage future boundary violations.

- **Limiting responses** reduces the narcissist's opportunity to provoke conflict.

- **Focusing on your children's well-being** provides the emotional motivation to stay calm and maintain peace, even in the most difficult situations.

Kerry's journey highlights the power of maintaining peace and control in the face of escalation. Her experience serves as a testament to the effectiveness of the strategies outlined in this chapter, reinforcing that with the right tools, you can successfully neutralize a narcissist's attempts to regain power.

Chapter Wrap-up

In this chapter, we explored the common escalation tactics that narcissists use when they sense they are losing control, such as guilt-tripping, playing the victim, triangulation, and sudden kindness (love-bombing). Recognizing these patterns is the first step toward maintaining your peace.

Key strategies for handling these provocations were outlined, including the Gray Rock Method for emotional detachment, maintaining clear and consistent boundaries, limiting responses to keep interactions brief and factual, and focusing on your children's well-being to stay grounded in your ultimate goal.

Additionally, we discussed the importance of avoiding re-engagement in conflict by refusing to justify yourself, sticking to the core issue, and employing the BIFF communication technique. By implementing these approaches, you can successfully prevent your narcissistic ex-partner from regaining emotional control.

Finally, building long-term resilience through self-care, surrounding yourself with a support system, and celebrating small victories were emphasized as crucial to sustaining peace in the face of future escalation attempts.

As you now understand the tools and strategies to maintain your peace during escalation attempts, the next step is to ensure that you continue to protect your emotional well-being and your children's. In the following chapter, we'll explore how you can help your children build emotional resilience in the face of the narcissistic co-parent's manipulations. By fostering their inner strength, you'll shield them from emotional harm and empower them to thrive despite the challenges they face.

Chapter 15

Sustaining Emotional Growth

"We are what we repeatedly do. Excellence, then, is not an act but a habit." — Aristotle

After completing the 60-day E.M.P.O.W.E.R. System, you've undoubtedly built emotional resilience, learned how to detach from conflict, and started to reclaim your life from the toxic influence of your narcissistic ex. But emotional growth does not end when you check off the final day of a program—it's a continuous process. This chapter is about ensuring that your progress is sustained over time, allowing you to avoid falling back into old emotional patterns and ensuring that you and your children remain emotionally protected.

To solidify the gains made through the E.M.P.O.W.E.R. System, we will explore key strategies for ongoing personal development, identify techniques to prevent backsliding into old habits, and highlight the importance of community and self-care in maintaining emotional strength.

Continued Personal Development

The work of personal growth doesn't end after you finish a system—it merely enters a new phase. Now that you've learned how to detach, regulate your emotions, and set boundaries, the next step is to ensure that these changes become permanent fixtures in your life. Sustaining emotional growth requires continuous learning and practice.

Here are some practical steps to keep growing after the 60-day system:

1. **Set New Goals for Emotional Growth:** Personal development doesn't end with detachment from conflict. Now that you've mastered the basics, it's time to set higher emotional goals. These might include improving your emotional intelligence, deepening your communication skills with your children, or learning how to cultivate joy even when external circumstances are challenging. Set specific, measurable goals that can guide your continued development.

2. **Daily Reflection and Journaling:** One of the most effective tools for maintaining growth is regular reflection. Journaling about your good and bad daily experiences allows you to track your progress and spot early signs of emotional backsliding. Writing down what triggers you, how you respond, and what strategies work best for you can be a powerful reminder of your growth.

3. **Practice Mindfulness and Meditation:** Building emotional resilience is not a one-time event but a daily practice. Incorporating

mindfulness or meditation into your routine helps you stay connected with your emotions in real-time, allowing you to respond thoughtfully rather than impulsively. Regular practice will make it easier to manage emotional triggers as they arise and prevent backsliding into old habits.

Preventing Backsliding into Old Patterns

It's natural to fear slipping back into old emotional cycles, especially when dealing with a manipulative ex-partner who might escalate their tactics when they see you growing stronger. It's important to recognize that emotional backsliding is a possibility but not a certainty. The key to avoiding this is being proactive in recognizing the signs and having strategies in place to counteract them.

- **Identify Your Emotional Triggers:** Even after the 60-day system, emotional triggers may still exist, especially if your ex continues to provoke or manipulate situations. Being aware of your specific triggers allows you to put distance between your emotions and your reactions. Practice pausing before you respond, using techniques like deep breathing or visualization to ground yourself in the present moment.

- **Revisit Your Boundaries:** Boundaries aren't set in stone—they need to evolve with you. Take the time to revisit the boundaries you've established with your ex. Are they still serving their purpose? Are there areas where you could be firmer or clearer? Adjusting your boundaries as needed ensures they continue to protect your emotional well-being, and consistently enforcing them will prevent backsliding.

- **Accountability and Support Systems:** One of the most effective ways to prevent slipping back into unhealthy emotional patterns is by enlisting the help of an accountability partner. This could be a trusted friend, family member, or therapist who understands your journey and can offer support. Having someone to check in with can help you stay on track and recognize early signs of emotional regression.

The Role of Self-Care in Emotional Growth

Self-care is often misunderstood as a luxury, but in reality, it's a necessity for anyone looking to maintain emotional strength and prevent burnout. Sustaining emotional growth requires consistent attention to your mental, physical, and emotional health. The more you nurture yourself, the more resilience you build against stress, conflict, and emotional manipulation.

- **Physical Self-Care:** Your body and mind are deeply connected. Regular physical activity, a healthy diet, and proper sleep are foundational to your emotional well-being. Exercise helps release pent-up stress and anxiety, while proper nutrition and rest provide the energy and mental clarity you need to navigate challenging situations calmly and calmly.

- **Emotional Self-Care:** Emotional self-care involves creating space to process your feelings without judgment. This can be done through activities like journaling, meditation, or simply talking to a trusted friend. The goal is to ensure that you're not suppressing your emotions, but instead allowing yourself to experience and release them in healthy ways.

- **Mental Self-Care:** Protecting your mental health is crucial for sustained growth. This includes limiting exposure to toxic influences, whether that's your ex's manipulative tactics or external stressors like social media. Engage in activities that stimulate your mind, such as reading, learning new skills, or engaging in hobbies that bring you joy and satisfaction.

Building and Maintaining a Support Network

One of the most powerful tools for maintaining emotional growth is building a support network. No one can sustain personal development in isolation. The people around you—whether friends, family, or a professional therapist—play a crucial role in reinforcing your emotional boundaries and encouraging continued growth.

- **Surround Yourself with Positive Influences:** It's vital to have people in your life who support your emotional journey and encourage you to grow. Seek out individuals who understand your situation and offer empathy, not judgment. Avoid those who may downplay your experiences or encourage you to revert to unhealthy behaviors.

- **Join Support Groups or Online Communities:** Many people have gone through similar experiences of co-parenting with a narcissistic ex. Joining a support group, whether in-person or online, can provide you with a sense of community and shared understanding. These groups offer valuable insights, emotional support, and a safe space to discuss your challenges and successes.

- **Professional Help:** Therapy or counseling can be an invaluable resource for ongoing emotional development. A therapist can help you identify areas for further growth, provide strategies for coping with stress, and offer support when dealing with setbacks. Don't hesitate to seek professional help, especially when dealing with complex emotions or mental health challenges.

Chapter Wrap-up

Sustaining emotional growth is not a one-time effort but a lifelong commitment. The strategies outlined in this chapter are designed to help you maintain your progress during the 60-day system and continue to grow emotionally long after it's over. Whether through daily mindfulness, revisiting your boundaries, or leaning on a support system, you now have the tools to stay empowered and protect your emotional well-being.

As you move forward, remember that growth is not always linear. There will be setbacks, but they don't define your journey. What matters most is your ability to get back on track using the skills and insights you've gained. With a strong foundation in self-care, support, and personal development, you are fully equipped to sustain long-term empowerment and peace.

As you continue to strengthen your emotional growth, it's essential to recognize that this journey isn't meant to be taken alone. While personal resilience and self-care are critical, the power of a strong, supportive community can amplify your progress and provide additional layers of protection against emotional setbacks. In the next chapter, we'll explore how to build and maintain a network of support that not only lifts you up but also reinforces the emotional boundaries and growth you've worked so hard to establish. Together, we'll look at the people and resources that can offer encouragement, guidance, and a sense of belonging as you navigate the ongoing challenges of co-parenting with a narcissist.

Chapter 16

Building a Supportive Community

"Connection is why we're here; it is what gives purpose and meaning to our lives." — Brené Brown

In times of emotional turmoil, we often forget how much strength lies in the connections we share with others. When you're co-parenting with a narcissistic ex-partner, isolation can feel like the only safe choice. But the reality is that trying to navigate these challenges alone can make the journey much harder. Building a supportive community allows you to access the guidance, empathy, and strength to carry you through the most difficult moments. This chapter will walk you through the process of cultivating a network of family, friends, and professionals to bolster your emotional resilience and help sustain your journey.

A supportive community isn't just a luxury—it's essential. You may hesitate to lean on others, fearing judgment or burdening those around you.

However, it's important to realize that a well-constructed support system isn't about burdening anyone; it's about mutual support. In fact, connecting with people who have experienced similar challenges can be a source of relief and validation. Emotional resilience is not something we build in isolation; it's developed through shared experiences, encouragement, and collective strength.

Now, let's explore how you can create this invaluable network and why it's so important for your emotional well-being and for fostering a stable environment for your children.

Identifying the Right People for Your Support Network

Building a support network begins by identifying who should be part of it. Not everyone in your life may be equipped to provide the support you need during this time. In fact, some people might unintentionally drain your emotional energy or make you feel worse about your situation. This is why it's crucial to surround yourself with those who genuinely care, have the emotional capacity to listen without judgment, and can offer guidance or simply be there to listen.

- **Family:** Close family members who understand the dynamics of your situation can be one of your strongest assets. They may have seen your challenges firsthand and can offer practical help with childcare, emotional support, or even help you navigate legal or financial matters.

- **Friends:** Long-term friends who have stood by you can be another great source of emotional strength. These people have seen you through ups and downs and can offer a sense of normalcy and perspective that might be difficult to find elsewhere.

- **Trusted Professionals:** Therapists, counselors, and legal professionals with experience in dealing with narcissistic behavior can offer specialized advice that can be pivotal to your success in co-parenting. These professionals can also help you develop strategies for maintaining your mental health and ensuring your children's safety and emotional well-being.

How Community Strengthens Emotional Resilience

When you're co-parenting with a narcissist, emotional resilience becomes a key skill you need to develop. Resilience isn't about being tough or unaffected by your situation. Instead, it's about being able to bounce back from setbacks, adapt to stressful circumstances, and maintain your well-being despite your challenges.

Building emotional resilience through community means you no longer carry the weight of your struggles alone. It allows you to tap into the collective strength of others, which can be incredibly empowering. Here's how community plays a role in fostering resilience:

- **Shared Experiences:** When you connect with others who have been through similar situations, you realize that you're not alone. This shared understanding can reduce feelings of isolation and validate your experiences. You'll find that hearing others' stories of navigating difficult co-parenting situations can offer insights and solutions you hadn't considered.

- **Emotional Outlet:** Having a safe space to express your frustrations, fears, and concerns can prevent the emotional buildup that leads to burnout. Knowing that someone is there to listen without judgment, whether a friend, a support group, or a therapist, can make an enormous difference in how you cope with daily challenges.

- **Perspective and Encouragement:** Sometimes, it's easy to get caught up in the day-to-day struggles of co-parenting with a narcissist. Your support network can offer fresh perspectives and encourage you to keep moving forward, even when it feels like progress is impossible. These positive reinforcements can help you stay focused on the long-term benefits of emotional detachment and boundary-setting.

Connecting with Others Who Understand Your Experience

There's immense value in connecting with people who understand exactly what you're going through. While friends and family are often supportive, they may not fully grasp the complexities of co-parenting with a narcissist. This is where support groups or online communities specifically tailored to individuals in similar situations can be incredibly beneficial.

Support groups, whether online or in person, offer a space to exchange stories, share advice, and receive emotional validation from others who have faced the same struggles. These groups often bring together people who have tried various approaches to co-parenting and can offer valuable insights into what works and what doesn't. Simply knowing that someone else has faced—and overcome—the same challenges can provide a powerful sense of hope.

Here are some ways to connect with others who share your experience:

- **Online Communities:** Platforms like Facebook, Reddit, and specialized forums host groups dedicated to people co-parenting with narcissists. These communities allow you to connect with others, share resources, and seek advice in a judgment-free environment.

- **Local Support Groups:** Many cities have local support groups for individuals dealing with narcissistic ex-partners. These groups often meet regularly and provide a structured environment where you can engage in discussions, attend workshops, or receive peer counseling.

- **Therapeutic Support:** Group therapy sessions that focus on narcissistic abuse or co-parenting challenges can also provide a deeper level of support. A licensed therapist guides these groups, offering professional insights while allowing participants to support one another.

Practical Steps to Build Your Support System

While building a supportive community sounds appealing, many people need help knowing where to start. Here are some practical steps you can take to begin cultivating your network:

1. **Reach Out to Trusted Individuals:** Start by identifying a few trusted family members or friends you feel comfortable sharing

your situation with. Set up regular check-ins, whether in person or over the phone, to talk about your challenges and victories. These conversations help you feel connected and grounded.

2. **Join a Support Group:** Find a local or online support group where you can interact with others facing similar challenges. Consider scheduling time weekly to engage with this group, as the consistency of interaction can help foster a stronger sense of community and belonging.

3. **Consult Professionals:** Seek out professionals like therapists, legal advisors, or co-parenting coaches who specialize in dealing with narcissistic ex-partners. Their expert guidance can be a critical piece of your support system, offering practical advice and emotional support tailored to your situation.

4. **Engage with Online Communities:** Don't underestimate the power of online communities. Join a few groups, participate in discussions, and ask questions when you feel stuck. You'll likely find others who have walked your path and are willing to share their knowledge and experiences.

Case Study: How Building a Supportive Community Transformed One Parent's Co-Parenting Journey

Melanie, a 38-year-old mother of two, had been co-parenting with her narcissistic ex-husband, Mark, for three years. The constant manipulation, boundary violations, and emotional turmoil were taking a toll on her well-being and her ability to provide a stable environment for her children. Melanie often felt isolated, believing no one could fully understand her situation. As a result, she kept her struggles to herself and tried to manage everything alone. Over time, this led to burnout, frustration, and emotional exhaustion.

Challenge: Melanie was dealing with several challenges:

1. **Emotional Isolation:** She lacked emotional support from people who understood what she was going through.

2. **Constant Conflict:** Her ex-husband thrived on creating conflict, and she didn't have the tools to disengage effectively.

3. **Impact on Her Children:** Melanie feared that the ongoing tension negatively affected her children, but she didn't know how to protect them emotionally.

4. **No External Support:** She had no professional guidance, such as a therapist or legal advisor, to help her navigate co-parenting with a narcissist.

Action: Melanie decided to take action and build a supportive community after realizing that trying to handle everything on her own was not sustainable. She followed a structured plan to create a network of emotional and professional support.

1. **Identifying Her Inner Circle:** Melanie began by reaching out to two close friends who had seen her through the ups and downs of her marriage and divorce. Although they didn't fully understand narcissistic abuse, they were willing to listen, offer emotional support, and help her manage the stress of co-parenting. She also opened up to her sister, who lived nearby, asking for help with the children when things became overwhelming.

2. **Joining an Online Community:** Melanie searched for online support groups and found a forum specifically for parents co-parenting with narcissists. Here, she discovered a network of people who had faced similar struggles. This community provided emotional validation and practical advice on handling difficult interactions with her ex. She started engaging with the group regularly, asking questions and sharing her own experiences. Through these discussions, she learned about the gray rock method—a technique to minimize her emotional responses to her ex's provocations.

3. **Seeking Professional Help:** Realizing she needed professional guidance, Melanie sought out a therapist who specialized in narcissistic abuse and co-parenting. The therapist helped her develop strategies for maintaining emotional detachment, setting firm boundaries, and managing her stress. Melanie also consulted with a family law attorney who provided legal advice on how to enforce her custody agreement when her ex attempted to violate it.

4. **Building a Routine of Support:** Melanie scheduled weekly check-ins with her two friends to discuss her progress and challenges. This routine gave her a sense of consistency and a safe space to express her frustrations. She also attended monthly group therapy sessions, where she could share her experiences and receive professional feedback on improving her co-parenting approach.

Outcome: Within three months, Melanie noticed significant improvements in her emotional resilience and co-parenting experience.

- **Reduced Emotional Stress:** Melanie felt less isolated after receiving support from her friends and online community. She no longer carried the emotional burden alone, and the validation she received from others made her feel understood and empowered. Using the Gray Rock Method, Melanie was able to respond to her ex-husband's manipulations with calm detachment. This reduced the amount of conflict and allowed her to maintain her peace.

- **Stronger Boundaries:** With her therapist's guidance, Melanie learned to set clear and enforceable boundaries. When her ex attempted to overstep or provoke her, she applied what she had learned in therapy to maintain emotional control and minimize her responses. Her lawyer helped her modify the custody agreement to include more specific guidelines for interactions, reducing her ex's opportunities for manipulation.

- **Improved Emotional Environment for Her Children:** Melanie's newfound emotional stability created a more peaceful home environment. Once tense and anxious during exchanges with their father, her children began to relax and feel more secure. She also taught them age-appropriate emotional resilience techniques, empowering them to cope with their father's behavior.

- **A Reliable Support System:** Melanie built a consistent and reliable support system by establishing regular check-ins with her friends, engaging in online discussions, and attending therapy. This network became her anchor during difficult moments, allowing her to navigate co-parenting with strength and confidence.

Conclusion: Melanie's case illustrates the transformative power of building a supportive community. By reaching out to trusted friends, engaging in an online community of like-minded individuals, and seeking professional guidance, she shifted from a state of emotional isolation to one of empowerment. Her experience underscores the importance of not going through the challenges of co-parenting with a narcissist alone. A strong support system helps reduce emotional stress and equips you with the tools to create a healthier environment for yourself and your children.

Chapter Wrap-up

At the heart of your emotional resilience lies your ability to build and rely on a supportive community. This chapter isn't just about connecting with others—it's about understanding that community is a lifeline during times of intense emotional struggle. Whether you're navigating a toxic co-parenting relationship or simply trying to maintain your emotional health, having a community that understands and supports you is essential.

By building a network of trusted family, friends, and professionals, you'll have the resources to maintain your boundaries, protect your well-being, and ensure that your children have a stable environment. Community support isn't a sign of weakness; it's a demonstration of your strength in knowing when to seek help.

Now that we've explored how to build a community of support, the next chapter will delve into the practicalities of maintaining your peace when your ex-partner tries to escalate the situation. Let's continue building the emotional tools you need to sustain a healthy co-parenting relationship.

Chapter 17

A Life of Empowerment Beyond the Narcissist

"You are not what happened to you. You are what you choose to become." — *Carl Jung*

In the wake of enduring the manipulative tactics and emotional strain that come with co-parenting with a narcissist, it can be difficult to imagine a future where peace, stability, and personal growth are at the forefront. But this chapter is designed to show you that not only is such a future attainable, but it's also your next step. Having completed the 60-day E.M.P.O.W.E.R. System journey, you now stand on the threshold of a new phase in your life—one filled with emotional freedom, clarity, and the ability to thrive beyond the daily struggles of co-parenting challenges.

It's time to explore how to turn your newfound strength into lasting empowerment, ensuring that you and your children continue to flourish.

Envisioning a Future Beyond Co-Parenting Challenges

The first step to long-term empowerment is to embrace the idea that your relationship with your narcissistic ex no longer defines your life. The co-parenting dynamic may remain, but the emotional grip they once held over you does not. You have now built the tools to keep their influence at a distance, and it's time to focus on what lies ahead—your growth, your healing, and your ability to create a healthy environment for your children.

Take a moment to reflect on your progress over the last 60 days. You've developed emotional resilience, learned to establish firm boundaries, and built practices that protect your well-being. The journey hasn't been easy, but every challenge has led you to this point—a place where you can confidently step forward and envision a future that isn't centered on conflict but on peace and personal empowerment.

Practical Tip: To help solidify this new vision, write down your goals for the future. What do you want for yourself and your children? These goals can be personal, professional, or related to your parenting. Having a clear vision helps reinforce that your focus is now on what you can control, not the chaos that once ruled your life.

Strategies for Sustaining Emotional Freedom

Emotional detachment from the narcissist has been the cornerstone of your progress, but maintaining this detachment requires ongoing commitment. As life presents new challenges, the narcissist in your life may continue to seek ways to regain control or provoke conflict. It's crucial to stay grounded in the practices you've learned and remain focused on the bigger picture—your freedom and the well-being of your children.

- **Reinforce Your Boundaries:** Boundaries are not set-and-forget tools; they require regular upkeep. Continue to enforce the boundaries you've put in place with your ex. Be consistent and unwavering in your communication, ensuring that you maintain control over how much access they have to your emotions.

- **Practice Emotional Regulation:** Even as you distance yourself from the narcissist's attempts to provoke you, emotional triggers may still surface, especially during significant events or stressful times. Mindfulness techniques and emotional regulation exercises, such as deep breathing, journaling, and reframing, will help you stay calm and focused.

- **Lean on Your Support System:** A solid support network has been instrumental in your progress thus far and will continue to be. Whether it's close friends, family, or a professional therapist, your support system can offer encouragement, perspective, and accountability as you continue on your path.

The work of emotional freedom doesn't end once the 60 days are over. You've built a foundation, but continued practice and self-awareness are essential to maintaining that freedom.

Ongoing Self-Care and Personal Development

Empowerment is not a static state; it's something you must nurture and grow over time. Now that you've gained the tools to manage your emotional responses and co-parent with confidence, it's time to turn your attention inward. Your emotional health and well-being are central to sustaining the progress you've made.

Self-care is more than just a momentary escape from stress; it's about creating habits that promote long-term well-being. Whether through regular exercise, meditation, or simply carving out time for hobbies and interests, nurturing yourself will replenish the emotional energy needed to stay grounded.

But beyond self-care, **personal development** is equally vital. This can take many forms: pursuing educational goals, expanding your career, or diving deeper into personal passions. Growth in these areas not only enhances your sense of fulfillment but also reinforces that you are more than the sum of your past experiences.

Practical Tip: Establish a weekly routine dedicated to personal development. This might include reading a book, attending a workshop, or simply dedicating time to reflect on your progress. Continuous learning and self-improvement keep you engaged in your growth journey and prevent stagnation.

Building a Future Focused on Hope and Empowerment

Now that you've mastered emotional detachment and re-established control over your life, it's time to set your sights on the future, where hope and empowerment guide every decision. The challenges of co-parenting with a narcissist will not disappear, but the way you handle them has fundamentally shifted.

- **Long-Term Resilience:** The resilience you've developed over the past 60 days will serve as your shield in moments of difficulty. Rather than reacting to provocations, you'll respond calmly, confident that you control your emotional world. This resilience will also be a guiding force for your children, modeling for them how to handle difficult situations with grace and strength.

- **Empowering Your Children:** As you step into your empowered future, your children will follow your lead. They've likely seen the transformation you've undergone, and they, too, will benefit from the peace and stability you've created. Continue to offer them guidance in managing their emotions, setting healthy boundaries, and maintaining a strong sense of self-worth, even in the face of their other parent's manipulations.

- **Redefining Your Identity:** This journey isn't just about co-parenting; it's about redefining who you are beyond the role of a parent. The strength, confidence, and emotional intelligence you've gained are tools that will enhance every aspect of your life. Whether it's your career, relationships, or personal fulfillment, you now have the power to shape your future on your terms.

Case Study: Reclaiming Emotional Freedom Through Detachment — Hailey's Journey Beyond Co-Parenting Challenges

Hailey, a 38-year-old mother of two, had been co-parenting with her narcissistic ex-husband, Jake, for three years. Their divorce had been tumultuous, marked by constant conflicts over parenting decisions, emotional manipulation, and repeated boundary violations. Every interaction with Jake left Hailey feeling emotionally drained and powerless. She found it challenging to focus on her well-being, as Jake's demands and provocations consumed her energy.

Hailey's main goal was to create a peaceful, emotionally stable environment for her children, free from the toxic dynamics that had dominated her life for years. However, she felt trapped in the cycle of conflict and manipulation, unsure how to detach herself emotionally while still being a responsible co-parent.

Challenges:

- **Constant Provocations:** Jake deliberately provoked Hailey by changing plans at the last minute, making demeaning comments about her parenting, and dragging her into unnecessary conflicts over trivial matters.

- **Difficulty Setting Boundaries:** Hailey had struggled to enforce firm boundaries with Jake, fearing that doing so might escalate the conflict or negatively affect her children.

- **Emotional Triggers:** Each interaction with Jake triggered a wave of anxiety, frustration, and guilt. Hailey found herself emotionally reacting to his provocations, which only fueled further conflict.

- **Children's Well-Being:** Hailey was deeply concerned about the impact this toxic dynamic had on her children, as they were frequently exposed to the tension between their parents.

Action: Hailey began implementing the E.M.P.O.W.E.R. System to regain control over her emotions and interactions with Jake. The system provided her with a structured approach to detachment and emotional regulation.

- **Emotional Regulation:** Hailey learned to identify her emotional triggers, recognizing that Jake's provocations were designed to elicit emotional reactions. By practicing mindfulness and deep breathing exercises, she began to regulate her responses, choosing calm over conflict. In moments of stress, she reminded herself that reacting emotionally only gave Jake more control over her.

- **Mindset Shift:** Hailey worked to shift her mindset from one of powerlessness to empowerment. She realized that while she couldn't change Jake's behavior, she had full control over how she responded to it. By reframing her thoughts, she moved from feeling like a victim of Jake's manipulation to an empowered co-parent who could protect her emotional space.

- **Boundary Setting:** One of Hailey's biggest breakthroughs came when she finally set clear, firm boundaries with Jake. She informed him that all communication regarding the children would be through email, except for emergencies. Hailey's decision to stick to this boundary reduced the number of unnecessary conflicts and allowed her to engage with Jake on her terms.

- **Gray Rock Method:** When Jake attempted to provoke Hailey through personal attacks or derogatory comments, she used the Gray Rock method—remaining emotionally unresponsive and giving neutral, brief replies. Over time, Jake's attempts at manipulation decreased as he realized that Hailey was no longer feeding into the conflict.

- **Self-Care and Resilience:** Hailey began prioritizing her well-being by dedicating time to self-care activities like journaling, yoga, and spending quality time with supportive friends and family. She also joined a support group for parents co-parenting with narcissists, where she found encouragement and advice from others in similar situations.

- **Children's Emotional Well-Being:** Hailey made a conscious effort to create a calm, nurturing home environment for her children. She taught them simple emotional regulation techniques, like deep breathing and journaling, to help them cope with any emotional stress they might feel. Hailey noticed a positive change in her children's behavior as the tension in their home decreased.

Results: Within two months of consistently applying the E.M.P.O.W.E.R. System, Hailey noticed a profound shift in her emotional state and her interactions with Jake:

- **Reduced Conflict:** By setting firm boundaries and detaching emotionally, Hailey drastically reduced the number of conflicts with Jake. Their interactions were now limited to essential parenting decisions, with minimal emotional engagement.

- **Emotional Freedom:** Hailey no longer felt consumed by the emotional turmoil Jake had once caused. She described feeling a sense of peace and control over her emotions, which allowed her to focus on her own well-being and the needs of her children.

- **Empowered Co-Parenting:** By shifting her mindset and enforcing boundaries, Hailey took back her power in the co-parenting relationship. She no longer reacted to Jake's provocations and was able to make decisions based on what was best for her and her children.

- **Children's Emotional Health:** Hailey's children began to thrive in the calmer environment she had created. They were less anxious, more open about their feelings, and more resilient when faced with challenges related to their father's behavior.

Key Takeaways:

- **Emotional Detachment:** Detaching from a narcissistic ex's provocations allows for more control and peace, without stepping away from parenting responsibilities.

- **Boundaries are Empowering:** Setting and enforcing boundaries, even in the face of resistance, is crucial for reclaiming emotional freedom.

- **Mindset Matters:** Shifting from a victim mentality to an empowered co-parent mindset fundamentally changes how you navigate the relationship.

- **Children Benefit:** Children thrive in an environment where their parents model emotional resilience and provide a peaceful, structured home.

Conclusion: Hailey's journey illustrates how the E.M.P.O.W.E.R. System can transform the co-parenting dynamic with a narcissist. By emotionally detaching, enforcing boundaries, and prioritizing her well-being, Hailey not only regained control over her life but also created a healthier, more stable environment for her children. Her story is a testament to the power of detachment as the key to long-term empowerment.

Chapter Wrap-up

As you close this chapter, know that your journey does not end here—it's just beginning. You've navigated some of the most challenging aspects of co-parenting with a narcissist, and you've emerged stronger, more resilient, and in control of your life. The strategies you've learned and the growth you've experienced will continue to serve you, not just in co-parenting, but in every facet of your life.

As you embark on this new chapter of your life, remember that the tools you've gained are just the beginning. Your path to lasting peace and emotional freedom is an ongoing journey—one that you now have the strength and insight to navigate with clarity.

Conclusion: Your Path to Lasting Peace

"The best way to predict the future is to create it." — *Peter Drucker*

In your journey through the E.M.P.O.W.E.R. System, you have explored a comprehensive approach to co-parenting with a narcissistic ex-partner. Each step has equipped you with tools to manage the emotional turmoil, set boundaries, and protect your children from the manipulative tactics often employed by a narcissist. You are no longer in the position you were at the beginning of this book—trapped in a cycle of conflict and manipulation. Instead, you now stand empowered, having mastered emotional detachment and control over your reactions. This final chapter solidifies the foundation you've built and inspires you to carry forward the lessons learned as you continue your co-parenting journey.

The core message of the E.M.P.O.W.E.R. System is simple: **detachment is your key to freedom and peace**. Through this framework, you have gained emotional resilience and the ability to protect both yourself and your children from the impact of narcissistic behavior. In this chapter, we will revisit the key insights of each element of the system, affirming the profound transformation you've undergone. By the end, you will not only feel a renewed sense of control but will also be prepared to maintain this peace long after the 60-day journey is complete.

Recap of the E.M.P.O.W.E.R. System

Each element of the E.M.P.O.W.E.R. System plays a vital role in shifting the power dynamic away from your ex and back to you. It has provided a structured roadmap for detaching from conflict, preserving your emotional health, and focusing on the well-being of your children.

Emotions: The first step was learning to identify and regulate your emotional responses. Narcissists thrive on eliciting emotional reactions because it gives them control. By recognizing your triggers and using techniques like mindfulness and deep breathing, you can now respond thoughtfully instead of impulsively. This emotional control has weakened your ex-partner's ability to manipulate you.

Mindset: Reframing your mentality from victimhood to empowerment was a crucial shift. You have learned to challenge negative thoughts and replace them with affirmations that reinforce your sense of control and self-worth. This mindset shift allowed you to see your role in the co-parenting relationship from a place of strength, focusing on what you can control rather than being overwhelmed by the narcissist's behavior.

Practices: Daily routines, including journaling, self-care, and meditation, have anchored you in emotional stability. These practices are more than just coping mechanisms—they are long-term strategies for maintaining your mental health and resilience. You've integrated them into your life, ensuring that even in moments of stress, you have tools to center yourself and protect your peace.

Obstacles: You've faced legal, financial, and emotional hurdles along the way, but the E.M.P.O.W.E.R. System has prepared you to navigate these challenges. You now anticipate the manipulative tactics your ex may use, and you have strategies in place to handle them. Whether documenting communication, seeking legal counsel, or relying on your support network, you're no longer blindsided by these obstacles.

Withdrawal: Detaching emotionally without disengaging from your parenting responsibilities was perhaps the most delicate balance to strike. You've learned techniques like the Gray Rock Method to minimize emotional responses during interactions with your ex. This withdrawal from conflict has allowed you to protect your mental health while still fulfilling your role as a parent.

Enforcement: Setting and enforcing boundaries is an ongoing process, but you now have the confidence to maintain them consistently. You've taken control of the co-parenting dynamic by practicing assertive communication and documenting violations. These boundaries are not just for your benefit; they also create a stable environment for your children, free from unnecessary conflict.

Resilience: Lastly, resilience is the thread that weaves everything together. You've built emotional strength not only for yourself but also for your children. Teaching them how to regulate their emotions and model resilience has ensured that they, too, are protected from the emotional fallout of the narcissistic parent. This resilience will serve you and your family for years to come, helping you navigate future challenges with grace and confidence.

Transformation Potential of the E.M.P.O.W.E.R. System

The transformation you've experienced is not just a surface-level change—it's a profound shift in how you engage with the world around you. You began this journey feeling trapped, emotionally drained, and overwhelmed by the narcissist's constant need for control. Now, you stand in a place of empowerment, having reclaimed control over your emotions, your reactions, and your life.

This transformation wasn't easy. It required dedication, self-reflection, and the courage to confront difficult truths. But with each passing day, you moved closer to the peace and stability you longed for. The E.M.P.O.W.E.R. System has shown you that detachment is not about giving up or surrendering control. Instead, it is about recognizing that true power lies in your ability to remain emotionally steady, regardless of external provocations.

As you continue to apply the principles of the E.M.P.O.W.E.R. System, you will find that this peace extends beyond your co-parenting relationship. Emotional regulation, resilience, and assertive boundary-setting are skills that can be applied to every area of your life—whether in personal relationships, professional settings, or even in your own self-talk. You are not just a better co-parent; you are a more empowered individual.

Reaffirming Emotional Strength and Peace

As you reflect on your journey, take a moment to acknowledge your growth. You've built a foundation of emotional strength that can withstand the storms of co-parenting with a narcissist. You've cultivated resilience in the face of manipulation, and you've learned to prioritize your own mental health and well-being. This strength is not temporary—it's a lasting change that will carry you forward.

Peace, however, does not mean the absence of challenges. There will be moments when your ex attempts to stir conflict or provoke an emotional reaction. But now, you have the tools to handle these moments calmly and clearly. You know how to set boundaries, protect your energy, and keep your focus on what truly matters—your children and your own well-being.

The power of the E.M.P.O.W.E.R. System lies in its ability to provide a clear path to lasting peace. You no longer have to feel like a victim of your circumstances. Instead, you are empowered to take control of your life and navigate the co-parenting relationship on your terms. This peace is not passive—it is an active choice you make every day to protect your emotional health and prioritize your family's well-being.

Moving Forward

As you close this book, remember that your journey does not end here. The principles of the E.M.P.O.W.E.R. System are tools you can return to time and again, especially when faced with new challenges. Continue to cultivate your emotional resilience, strengthen your boundaries, and prioritize your peace. The road ahead may still present difficulties, but you now have the confidence and clarity to handle whatever comes your way.

Look to the future with hope. The emotional freedom you've gained through this journey is the foundation upon which you will build a peaceful, stable, and fulfilling life. You've already proven that you have the strength to navigate the most difficult situations, and now, you have the tools to sustain that strength for the long term.

As you move forward, trust in the process. Trust in your ability to maintain peace, no matter what challenges arise. Most importantly, trust in the transformation you've experienced—the transformation that has made you a more empowered parent, a stronger individual, and a person who no longer needs to engage in conflict to feel in control.

I'd Love Your Feedback!

Thank you for joining me on this journey through *Quitting to Win: Master Co-parenting with a Narcissist in 60 Days with the E.M.P.O.W.E.R. System*. I hope this book has offered you valuable tools, insights, and inspiration to build a peaceful and empowering co-parenting relationship.

If this book has helped you in any way, I'd be grateful if you could take a moment to leave a review. Your feedback not only helps other readers discover practical solutions for similar challenges but also allows me to keep improving resources and guidance.

How to Leave a Review:

1. **Visit the Book's Product Page:** You can find the book on your Amazon orders page.

2. **Share Your Honest Thoughts:** Whether a single strategy or a powerful insight resonated with you, I'd love to hear how this book impacted your life.

3. **Provide a Star Rating:** Ratings help others gauge the value of the book, so every rating counts!

What to Mention in Your Review

- Which part of the E.M.P.O.W.E.R. System made the biggest difference?

- How has the book helped you approach co-parenting challenges?

- Are there any specific tools or chapters that stood out to you?

Your review, however brief, will mean a lot. It's one of the best ways to support our mission of helping more parents find peace and empowerment in their co-parenting journey.

Thank you again for trusting us with this part of your journey. I wish you continued strength, resilience, and lasting peace!

References

American Psychiatric Association. (2013). Diagnostic and statistical manual of mental disorders (5th ed.). Arlington, VA: American Psychiatric Publishing.

Caligor, E., Levy, K. N., & Yeomans, F. E. (2015). Narcissistic personality disorder: Diagnostic and clinical challenges. American Journal of Psychiatry, 172(5), 415-422.

Couples, A. (2024). Narcissistic relationship. AllyCouples. Retrieved October 1, 2024, from https://allycouples.com/blog/narcissistic-relationship

Kacel, E. L., Ennis, N., & Pereira, D. B. (2017). Narcissistic personality disorder in clinical health psychology practice: Case studies of comorbid psychological distress and life-limiting illness. Behavioral Medicine, 43(3), 156-164.

McLean Hospital. (n.d.). Narcissistic personality disorder: A basic guide for providers. Retrieved October 1, 2024, from https://www.mcleanhospital.org/npd-provider-guide

Beckmeyer, J. J., Coleman, M., & Ganong, L. H. (2014). Postdivorce co-parenting typologies and children's adjustment. Family Relations, 63(4), 526-537.

Feinberg, M. E. (2003). The internal structure and ecological context of co-parenting: A framework for research and intervention. Parenting: Science and Practice, 3(2), 95-131.

The Firm on Baltimore PLLC. (2023, July 14). Child custody matters: Tips for co-parenting successfully. https://lawtulsa.com/2023/07/14/child-custody-matters-tips-for-co-parenting-successfully/

American Psychological Association. (2012). Guidelines for the practice of parenting coordination. American Psychologist, 67(1), 63-71.

Feinberg, M. E. (2001). Coparenting and the transition to parenthood: A framework for prevention. Clinical Child and Family Psychology Review, 4(4), 319-344.

Bradberry, T., & Greaves, J. (2009). Emotional Intelligence 2.0. TalentSmart.

Goleman, D. (2007). Emotional Intelligence (10th ed.). Bantam Books.

Manhattan Mental Health Counseling. (n.d.). 5 Emotional Regulation Skills.

Perchtold-Stefan, C. M., Papousek, I., Fink, A., Weiss, E. M., & Rominger, C. (2023). Emotional regulation strategies in daily life: the intensity of emotions matters. Frontiers in Psychology, 14.

Raypole, C. (2022, September 29). Emotional Regulation Skills: Learn How to Manage Your Emotions. Psych Central.

McNulty Counseling. (n.d.). Navigating the stormy waters of co-parenting with a narcissist. Retrieved October 3, 2024, from

Raypole, C. (2022, February 23). How to co-parent with someone with narcissistic traits: 5 tips. Psych Central.

Trust Mental Health. (n.d.). Co-parenting with a narcissist: A guide. Retrieved October 3, 2024, from

Wilkinson, K. (n.d.). How to support your partner when they're co-parenting with a narcissist ex. Blended Family Frappe. Retrieved October 3, 2024, from

Katz-Wise, S. L., Priess, H. A., & Hyde, J. S. (2021). Keeping Your Coparent in Mind: A Longitudinal Investigation of Mindfulness in Coparenting. Mindfulness, 12(8), 1956-1968. https://doi.org/10.1007/s12671-021-01658-w

Parent, J., McKee, L. G., N Rough, J., & Forehand, R. (2016). The Association of Parent Mindfulness with Parenting and Youth Psychopathology Across Three Developmental Stages. Journal of Abnormal Child Psychology, 44(1), 191-202.

Collaborative Divorce Golden Gate. (2024, July 2). Mindful Co-Parenting – Importance of Mindfulness Tools.

Yeh, K. (n.d.). Grow Your Mindfulness and Self-Compassion Skills through Journaling. Parent Self Care.

Holleron, A. J. (n.d.). Using mindfulness to manage emotions of parenting and co-parenting.

Evans, M. T. (n.d.). You can thrive after narcissistic abuse. Retrieved October 3, 2024, from

Legg, T. J. (2022, February 23). How to co-parent with someone with narcissistic traits: 5 tips. PsychCentral.

Raypole, C. (2022, September 30). Co-parenting with a narcissist. Medical News Today.

WebMD. (n.d.). What to do if you're co-parenting with a narcissist. Retrieved October 3, 2024, from

JudgeAnthony.com. (n.d.). Co-parenting with a narcissist: What you need to know! JudgeAnthony.com.

Talkspace. (n.d.). Co-parenting with a narcissist: Tips for navigating. Talkspace.

Steele Family Law. (n.d.). 10 survival tips for co-parenting with a narcissist. Steele Family Law.

McNulty Counseling and Wellness. (n.d.). Navigating the stormy waters of co-parenting with a narcissist. McNulty Counseling and Wellness.

Casanova, M. (n.d.). The importance of boundaries in co-parenting. Our Family Wizard Blog. Retrieved from

Eddy, B. (2019). BIFF for co-parent communication: Your guide to difficult texts, emails, and social media posts. Unhooked Books.

Gottman, J., & Silver, N. (2015). The seven principles for making marriage work: A practical guide from the country's foremost relationship expert. Harmony.

McBride, K. (2016). Will I ever be free of you?: How to navigate a high-conflict divorce from a narcissist and heal your family. Atria Books.

Warshak, R. A. (2011). Divorce poison: How to protect your family from bad-mouthing and brainwashing. William Morrow Paperbacks.

Brantley, H. T. (2011). Cultivating a role in parenting coordination. Good Practice, Spring 2011, 10-11. American Psychological Association.

Farzad, B. (n.d.). Top 9 communication techniques for successful co-parenting. Farzad Family Law.

Lamela, D., Figueiredo, B., Morais, A., Matos, P., & Jongenelen, I. (2021). Parenting styles, coparenting, and early child adjustment in separated/divorced families with sole or joint physical custody processes ongoing in court. International Journal of Environmental

Research and Public Health, 18(15), 8034.

Martínez-Pampliega, A., Cormenzana, S., Corral, S., Iraurgi, I., & Sanz, M. (2022). Indicators of child victimization in high-conflict divorce. Anuario de Psicología Jurídica, 32(1), 71-79.

Visser, M., Finkenauer, C., Schoemaker, K., Kluwer, E., Rijken, R. V., Lawick, J. V., Bom, H., Schipper, J. C., & Lamers-Winkelman, F. (2022). Healing the separation in high-conflict post-divorce co-parenting. Frontiers in Psychology, 13, 891134.

American Psychological Association. (2012). Building your resilience.

Southwick, S. M., Bonanno, G. A., Masten, A. S., Panter-Brick, C., & Yehuda, R. (2014). Resilience definitions, theory, and challenges: Interdisciplinary perspectives. European Journal of Psychotraumatology, 5(1), 25338.

Masten, A. S. (2001). Ordinary magic: Resilience processes in development. American Psychologist, 56(3), 227-238.

Tugade, M. M., & Fredrickson, B. L. (2004). Resilient individuals use positive emotions to bounce back from negative emotional experiences. Journal of Personality and Social Psychology, 86(2), 320-333.

Reivich, K., & Shatté, A. (2002). The resilience factor: 7 essential skills for overcoming life's inevitable obstacles. Broadway Books.

American Psychological Association. (2012). Building your resilience. Retrieved from

Bonanno, G. A., Westphal, M., & Mancini, A. D. (2011). Resilience to loss and potential trauma. Annual Review of Clinical Psychology, 7, 511-535.

Masten, A. S. (2001). Ordinary magic: Resilience processes in development. American Psychologist, 56(3), 227-238.

Southwick, S. M., Bonanno, G. A., Masten, A. S., Panter-Brick, C., & Yehuda, R. (2014). Resilience definitions, theory, and challenges: Interdisciplinary perspectives. European Journal of Psychotraumatology, 5(1), 25338.

Sillick, T. J., & Schutte, N. S. (2006). Emotional intelligence and self-esteem mediate between perceived early parental love and adult happiness. E-Journal of Applied Psychology, 2(2), 38-48. Retrieved from

Masten, A. S., & Barnes, A. J. (2018). Resilience in children: Developmental perspectives. Children, 5(7), 98.

Michigan State University Extension. (2014, March 6). Help kids develop resiliency across the ages and stages of their lives.

Pinto, T. M., Laurence, P. G., & Macedo, C. R. (2021). Resilience programs for children and adolescents: A systematic review and meta-analysis. Frontiers in Psychology, 12, 543477.

Weir, K. (2017). Maximizing children's resilience. Monitor on Psychology, 48(8), 40.

Birkley, E. L., & Eckhardt, C. I. (2015). Anger, hostility, internalizing negative emotions, and intimate partner violence perpetration: A meta-analytic review. Clinical Psychology Review, 37, 40-56.

Greenberg, L. S. (2015). Emotion-focused therapy: Coaching clients to work through their feelings. American Psychological Association.

Kross, E., & Ayduk, O. (2017). Self-distancing: Theory, research, and current directions. Advances in Experimental Social Psychology, 55, 81-136.

Neff, K. D., & Germer, C. K. (2013). A pilot study and randomized controlled trial of the mindful self-compassion program. Journal of Clinical Psychology, 69(1), 28-44.

Fredrickson, B. L. (2001). The role of positive emotions in positive psychology: The broaden-and-build theory of positive emotions. American Psychologist, 56(3), 218-226.

Neff, K. D., & Germer, C. K. (2013). A pilot study and randomized controlled trial of the mindful self-compassion program. Journal of Clinical Psychology, 69(1), 28-44.

Seligman, M. E., Steen, T. A., Park, N., & Peterson, C. (2005). Positive psychology progress: Empirical validation of interventions. American Psychologist, 60(5), 410-421